W9-BPE-229

3 1310 0026

Praise for *Talking Back to Dr. Phil* . . .

"David Bedrick takes on Dr. Phil in a intelligent, sensitive way that readers will find enlightening and validating. He uses Dr. Phil as a foil to give expression to a deeper, more comprehensive understanding of hot issues like race, gender, diet, sex, and power relationships. Here is the Anti-Dr. Phil—at last, someone who can stand up knowledgeably to Dr. Phil's suave bullying."

—Robert W. Fuller, Ph.D.
Former president of Oberlin College and author of *Somebodies and Nobodies* and
Religion and Science

"At last someone is taking on Dr. Phil with good sense and great humor. Life isn't a sixty-minute show where people just come in for the laying on of hands. Life is about working it all out with family, community, and love. Good for Mr. Bedrick to decide to pull off the gloves and have an emotional slugfest with an over-the-high-school bully. *Talking Back to Dr. Phil* is a must read. But not at dinnertime ... you'll be laughing too hard to eat."

—Nikki Giovanni
Poet

"David Bedrick understands that real change or transformation requires challenging accepted dogma and then approaching problems with compassion and curiosity. A great advocate for stopping the madness of body hatred and dieting."

—Jane R. Hirschmann and Carol H. Munter
Authors of *Overcoming Overeating* and *When Women Stop Hating Their Bodies*

"In *Talking Back to Dr. Phil*, David Bedrick contrasts mainstream mental health and psychology with a new approach based on love and radical belief. Main stream psychology tells us we are sick, bad, or wrong. But for Bedrick our fatigues, aches, pains, anxieties, low moods, and even the difficulties we encounter in our jobs and relationships, are all educational and growing opportunities with out which we would not develop more awareness. I agree with Bedrick that our sickness deserves our love because it contains the medicine toward our wholeness and well-being."

—Pierre Morin, M.D., Ph.D.
Coauthor of *Inside Coma* and
clinical director of Lutheran Community Services

"In *Talking Back to Dr. Phil*, David Bedrick gets it right. He isn't talking back just to Dr. Phil but to a whole century of normative psychology, an approach to mental health that has more to do with socialization than with well-being. Bedrick adds a crucial missing piece to the equation: love. Not just ordinary love but love of our uniqueness, diversity, and struggles—a kind of love sorely missing in mainstream psychology. A modern-day Walt Whitman, Bedrick sings the beauty of our humanity and exhorts us to do the same, to prize the deepest levels of our diversity and express the many wonderful, crazy, and colorful ways there are of being human."

—Julie Diamond, Ph.D.
Organizational consultant, coach, and coauthor of
A Path Made by Walking

"David Bedrick has written an articulate and thought-provoking book challenging the conventional applications of mainstream psychology. His writing introduces the reader to a love-based psychology that embraces personal challenges with care and consideration and offers the possibility that insight can be gained through exploring the difficulties themselves. His work is a valuable and refreshing contribution to the field of psychology and is an invitation to each of us to embrace all that we are and, in so doing, become all that we may be."

—Stephen Schuitevoerder, Ph.D.
International consultant and president of the Process Work Institute

"When it comes to domestic violence, the silence of physicians, therapists, counselors, clerics, parents, and even prosecutors and judges must end. Mr. Bedrick's plea for seeing this complex familial problem with clarity and genuine compassion is indispensable to any progress in helping victims protect themselves rather than our current practice of blaming them."

—Elizabeth Welch
Senior Circuit Court Judge, Portland, Oregon

"This groundbreaking book demystifies mainstream psychology by calling out Dr. Phil, showing not only the limitations of his approach, which seeks to restore and maintain 'normal' behavior, but how it perpetuates a mode of psychologizing that reinforces the very pathology it purports to heal. David Bedrick reveals symptoms as allies assisting in growth and insight rather than as signs of sickness or deviations from a norm. And rather than focus only on individuals, he demonstrates how society fosters disturbances that, when processed, contribute to transforming not only the individuals but their relationships, groups, and potentially society itself. As such, Bedrick offers new directions for addressing some of the most perplexing issues of our time, from lying and pornography to addiction and racism."

—Herbert D. Long, Th.D., Dipl. PW
Former dean and Francis Greenwood Peabody lecturer, Harvard University
Divinity School, and adjunct faculty member, Marylhurst University

"*Talking Back to Dr. Phil* gives us a new vision of psychology, one where people are seen not as functional or dysfunctional but in terms of their diversity, and where awareness and dialogue are more important than labels. When people are supported to express their deepest hopes, dreams, and fears, they become reconnected to their humanity and we take one step closer to creating a beloved community. A breath of fresh air."

—Vassiliki Katrivanou, M.A.
Member of the Greek Parliament, therapist, and Mediation and
Conflict Resolution trainer

"*Talking Back to Dr. Phil* is a breath of fresh air to those who have been hurt and put down by the righteous morality and shame of popular psychology. Bedrick, in daring to pull back the veil of the status quo, reveals an approach that invites self-discovery, finds meaning and purpose in problems, and values the social challenges of our times. Anyone who longs for the freedom of their own individual path of heart will be uplifted by this book."

—Dawn Menken, Ph.D.
Psychotherapist and author of *Speak Out! Talking about Love, Sex and Eternity*

"*Talking Back to Dr. Phil* is full of humor, wisdom, and compassion. Bedrick takes a fresh, holistic approach to psychology, recognizing that feelings are not to be repressed and overcome but actually provide a pathway into deep healing."

—Jennifer Means, N.D., M.Ac.O.M.

"Remarkable! Bedrick's perspective on dieting and weight loss gave me goose bumps."

—Marlene M. Maheu, Ph.D.
Editor-in-chief of *Self Help Magazine*, lead author of *The Mental Health Professional and the New Technologies*, and executive director of the Telemental Health Institute

"For many women, it is revolutionary to realize that what will silence the accusatory inner body-image voice isn't losing weight but rather listening to the body's wisdom. It could definitely be said that the essays on diet and body image in this book are a work of Spirit through and through."

—Andrea Hollingsworth, Ph.D.
Assistant professor of Christian Thought, Berry College

Talking Back to
Dr. Phil

Alternatives to

Mainstream Psychology

David Bedrick
J.D., Dipl. PW
Foreword by Arnold Mindell, Ph.D.

BELLY ● SONG
press
Santa Fe, New Mexico

Published by: Belly Song Press
                518 Old Santa Fe Trail
                Suite 1 #626
                Santa Fe, NM 87505
                www.bellysongpress.com

Editor: Ellen Kleiner
Book design and production: Ann Lowe
Cover image: Ann Lowe

Copyright © 2013 by David Bedrick

No part of this book may be reproduced, stored, or transmitted in any form or by any means except for brief quotations in reviews or for purposes of criticism, commentary, or scholarship without written permission from the publisher.

Talking Back to Dr. Phil is factually accurate, except that names, locales, and minor aspects of some essays have been altered to preserve coherence while protecting privacy.

Printed in the United States of America on recycled paper

PUBLISHER'S CATALOGING-IN-PUBLICATION DATA
Bedrick, David.

   Talking back to Dr. Phil : alternatives to mainstream psychology /
   David Bedrick ; foreword by Arnold Mindell. -- Santa Fe, N.M. : Belly Song Press, c2013.

      p. ; cm.

      ISBN: 978-0-9852667-0-7 (print) ; 978-0-9852667-1-4 (ebk.)
      Includes bibliographical references and index.
      Summary: A critique of mainstream psychology's ineffectiveness, neglect of the personal and social meaning behind people's suffering, lack of diversity-mindedness, and predisposition to shame rather than understand people. It takes Dr. Phil as a representative, a straw man, for this kind of thinking. Discussing sixteen specific episodes of the Dr. Phil show, the book provides alternative perspectives on such topics as lying, judging, labeling, dieting, anger, shame, addictions, relationships, domestic violence, race, and gender.

      1. Psychology--Philosophy. 2. McGraw, Phillip C., 1950-3. Mental health counseling--Practice. 4. Social psychology. 5. Suffering--Psychological aspects. 6. Self-help techniques. 7. Sexism--Psychological aspects. 8. Self-actualization (Psychology) I. Title. II. Title: Alternatives to mainstream psychology.

BF38 .B43 2013   2012914866
150.1--dc23   1302

1 3 5 7 9 10 8 6 4 2

To dreams,
dreaming,
and the dreaming earth

Acknowledgments

ABOUT TWENTY-FIVE YEARS AGO, I had the privilege of hearing the music and poetry of Etheridge Knight, a freedom-loving black poet living in Boston. I contacted him years later knowing he would not remember me; nonetheless, he invited me to his home, where he recited his poems and made up new ones for me, including "We struggle to be, we struggle to be free. Me, thee, and we." I explained that "Belly Song," the title poem of one of his books, was near and dear to me, whereupon he asked me to "tell it." I shyly began to speak the three pages of poetry from memory. His leathery face, worn from racism, prison, drugs, and alcohol, streamed with his tears. "You own that poem; I give it to you," he said. His gift left me feeling worthy of writing.

I am forever grateful to him and to my many great teachers, including Arny and Amy Mindell, Max Schupbach, Salome Schwarz, and Jerry Fjerkenstad, all of whom have helped me unfold my dreams and shown me the spiritual and psychological power of process-oriented psychology. The worldwide Process Work community of teachers and therapists has laid before me the workings of a world in love and compassion as well as in war and in conflict; I am deeply indebted to these women and men.

And I am humbled by the generosity of Markus Marty, whose process of dying of AIDS healed me and many others; by Makwa, whose indigenous nature endured great suffering even as he sang my name to me; and by Renae Hanson, who helped me come to know my story.

In addition, I extend gratitude to African American educators, writers, and activists Cornel West, James Baldwin, Maya Angelou, Nikki Giovanni, bell hooks, and Howard Thurman, who have taught me that justice is love in action, love in the world. This book represents my voice informed by their mission.

I also appreciate the impressive work of Ellen Kleiner, my editor, who loved this manuscript enough to challenge it, critique it, and craft it for publication. She knew I was pregnant and steadily midwifed the medium of my message through its sometimes arduous passage.

Then, too, my mother and father, both deceased, sacrificed some of their own dreams so that mine could be realized. My father called me a "dreamer," and my mother told me to stop trying to change the world; subsequently I became a dream analyst and activist. Still, they "saw" me and their words found their proper place in me. Now my dreams have become theirs.

My deepest gratitude and love extend to my wife Lisa, my best friend, who has created beauty, sweetness, joy, and tenderness during the years it took to make this book a reality. She has read each sentence and citation countless times, lovingly holding my hand amidst challenges and celebrating each moment of accomplishment.

Contents

Foreword

PSYCHOLOGY NEEDS NEW BLOOD. *Talking Back to Dr. Phil* provides just that. It offers a sense of magic and good feeling behind the veil of psychological labeling to reveal the meaning behind people's suffering. Its scope is wide-ranging, encompassing many issues of interest to practitioners of psychology, as well as to ordinary people in contemporary society who seek a better understanding of their problems and behaviors. It tackles the issue of domestic violence, focusing not only on victims and perpetrators but on the role our culture plays by denying pain and insisting that people appear happy. It takes on the issue of weight loss, standing up for women's sense of beauty and empowerment against a $60 billion diet industry. It deals with relationship conflict, a topic many try to get around by recommending compromise and harmony without getting to the guts of the deeper problems people face. It breaks new ground in essays on addictions and obsessions, exploring the deep reasons people use substances instead of viewing them as quick fixes and delivering moral critiques. Its commitment to social justice shines through in chapters on race and education; gender, age, and sexuality; and family diversity.

David Bedrick is the ideal guide who masters both the realist's and the dreamer's overview of today's world. He is a fierce advocate of diversity both in our global community and in ourselves. His background as an attorney, therapist, and teacher are evident in this book, but behind the words, critiques, and new solutions offered are a deep love and tenderness toward people and the difficulties they suffer. *Talking Back to Dr. Phil* is a fun, psychologically educational, and brilliant yet easy-to-read book that dives into the essence and emerges with loving and realistic advice about everyday life.

Thank you, David, for making this rich and accessible contribution to the understanding of ourselves and the world around us.

—Arnold Mindell, Ph.D.

Yachats, Oregon

Introduction

*It is more interesting, more complicated, more intellectually demanding
and more morally demanding to love somebody, to take care of somebody,
to make one other person feel good.*

—Toni Morrison

THE PURPOSE OF *Talking Back to Dr. Phil* is to further a dialogue about
the role and practice of psychology in today's society. In our modern
culture, everyone practices psychology. Psychological thinking is so woven
into our day-to-day lives that we attribute almost everything disturbing
to us about ourselves or others to a psychological problem in need of
diagnosis and treatment. When we experience disturbing feelings, we say
we are depressed, hot tempered, overly sensitive, insecure, or have low self-
esteem. When we become aware of disturbing patterns of behavior, we say
we are lazy, undisciplined, out of control, self-medicating, or judgmental.
We also show this predilection for diagnosing when we are disturbed by
other people's emotions and behaviors, assuming that they have anger issues,
lack self-control, are egotistical, narcissistic, out of touch, depressed, irresponsible, or lazy. We even diagnose whole groups of people who disturb us,
concluding that they are immoral, oversexed, greedy, menacing, manipulative,
untrustworthy, irresponsible, or criminal.

Supporting the practice of this kind of psychology are many professional analysts and scores of books, magazines, Internet sites, and television

programs suggesting ways to rid people of disturbing feelings and behavior patterns, all the while bombarding us with messages that we are in need of correction or reprogramming. Such sources guide us to stop eating certain foods or ingesting certain substances, as if there were nothing to learn from exploring our yearnings; to stop making certain choices, as if there were no deeper reasons for our actions; to antidepress, as if emotions that move us into ourselves have nothing to offer us. We are told, "Stop eating that," "Don't worry so much," "Don't judge," "Forgive, apologize," "Be honest," "Make different choices," "Don't be so aggressive (sensitive, passive, cold, bold, insecure)," "Don't act on your attraction to certain people," "Stop falling in love with the wrong people," "Be more reasonable (rational, normal)." However, such psychological platitudes focusing on individuals' inadequacies rarely address the issues underlying people's behaviors or offer ways to deepen personal transformation.

THE APPROACH OF MAINSTREAM PSYCHOLOGY

The average person, your own naive unconsciousness, leads you to believe that medicine will heal your body, that psychology will make you more reasonable, and that being nice will help you win your relationships problems.
— Arnold Mindell

The powerful habit we have all learned of viewing aspects of ourselves and others that disturb us as inadequacies or pathologies to be corrected I call the practice of "mainstream psychology." Mainstream psychology, with its roots in allopathic medicine, regards people's difficulties as symptoms of illness, and feelings and behaviors outside the norm as needing to be suppressed or eliminated—instead of exploring their underlying meanings for information that could aid in personal transformation and seeing beauty, power, and intelligence in their diversity. In essence, it meets what disturbs people with the simple question "What is wrong with them?" In the process of doing so, mainstream psychology often discards the seeds of more authentic lives, more sustainable relationships, and more enlightened communities.

The norms inherent in mainstream psychology's diagnoses essentially reflect the majority's values, beliefs, and viewpoints regarding psychological health. As such, it is a psychology often in service of normalizing people, seeking to help them act more reasonably and get along better with others even when accommodation is contrary to their natures and life paths. In these ways, mainstream psychology ignores the role psychology can play in helping people find meaning and power in their difficulties, make contact with the magic and mystical elements of life, and be nurtured by their uniqueness and diversity.

AN ALTERNATIVE TO MAINSTREAM PSYCHOLOGY— A LOVE-BASED PSYCHOLOGY

You are who you are because somebody loved you.
—Cornel West

An alternative to mainstream psychology is a love-based psychology that views people, including their disturbing feelings and behaviors, as a reflection of nature's diversity. We look upon nature—bees building and sustaining their hives, bats eating fruit and reseeding forests, worms aerating the earth, birds performing a colorful mating dance—and marvel at the beauty, power, and intelligence in the diversity of nature down to its smallest details. It is as if, in the words of poet William Butler Yeats, "every thing we look upon is blest."[1] The awe the natural world inspires moves us to carefully observe it, caringly protect it, and reach to it for solace and communion. We don't try to correct nature's diversity of expression so that it conforms to our views of preferred behavior or activities. We don't see a winter that lingers on as lazy or an unexpected storm as undisciplined but accept and appreciate the varied seasons and forces inherent in nature. We see the natural world's expressions—every color, shape, sound, and pattern of behavior—as imbued with meaning and the potential for evolution.

Consequently, since people are part of nature and exhibit diverse qualities informed by the same intelligence we attribute to the natural world, it follows that even the most disturbing feelings and behaviors exhibited by people have meaning that we can discover by exploring them rather than repudiating them. This alternative approach, which I consider a love-based psychology, is less inclined to perceive people's difficulties as pathological or aim to fix people than to look for meaning in difficulties, an underlying order in what appears to be chaos, and expressions of spirit in actions that appear to be unworthy of compassion or understanding. In *Talking Back to Dr. Phil*, which is predicated on such an approach, I draw on process-oriented psychology, Jungian psychology, feminist psychology, systems theory, quantum physics, Zen Buddhism, Taoism, African-American history, and lessons I have learned from clients and students to look not only at people's behaviors but at social issues from a perspective that reflects a love-based psychology.

THE PRACTICE OF A LOVE-BASED PSYCHOLOGY

A flower is moral by its own flowering.
—Etheridge Knight

Seeing people as part of nature and considering what appears different and disturbing with compassion is the basis for the practice of a love-based psychology. Unfortunately, too often we react to feelings and behaviors we find disagreeable by judging them and shaming individuals who exhibit them, implying that these aspects of ourselves and others are the result of inadequacies that need analysis and treatment. Why am I like this? Why do I keep doing this? Why do I feel this way? Why are those people like that? Why don't they act more appropriately? are common responses of those who have been shamed into thinking something is wrong with them or who have taken up the mantle of shaming others. People spend countless hours, years, or even their whole lives bowing before the altar of shame.

By contrast, a love-based psychology views people and their difficulties through a lens of love. Like a naturalist, who assumes that nature reflects order, intelligence, and beauty, those with the perspective of a love-based psychology assess people's feelings and behaviors with respect, compassion, and radical belief rather than judgment. Respect, as the word implies, is the willingness to look (thus the root "spect") and then look again (thus the prefix "re"). Respect entails a careful and caring examination of people's experiences, precluding a rush to diagnosis, awakening curiosity about what is observed and how it might reflect their deeper needs and potential for transformation. Compassion guides this loving examination, resulting in appreciation for people's experiences and an inclination to resist judging, stereotyping, and marginalizing what might be deemed disagreeable. Radical belief is the faith that even our greatest difficulties and most disturbing behaviors are meaningful and informed by intelligence—and thus contain the seeds of important future developments.

PRINCIPLES OF A LOVE-BASED PSYCHOLOGY

Love transforms with redemptive power.
—Martin Luther King Jr.

The following principles underlie the practice of a love-based psychology. One or more of these principles is embodied in the alternatives to mainstream psychology discussed in each essay of this book.

Principle 1: **A love-based psychology deals with the structure and details of people's difficulties, whether internal or external, as reflecting important knowledge about changes they need or hope to make.**

A love-based psychology treats the details of people's struggles, such as foods they want to stop eating, types of individuals they'd like to dissociate from in their lives and dreams, habits they hope to break, physical symptoms from which they suffer, and feelings they want to eliminate, as if they form a crucible for growth out of which can come solutions to people's problems and answers to their life questions.

By contrast, mainstream psychology, like allopathic medicine, views such details as indicative of inadequacies or pathologies to be suppressed or eliminated. That is, mainstream psychology seeks to help people leave bad relationships, abstain from bad habits, and overcome painful feelings without taking into account the intelligence and meaning behind these predicaments and the possibilities their investigation offers for growth.

Principle 2: **A love-based psychology treats things that disturb people about themselves or others as revelations of their deeper nature.**

Transformation and healing require upsetting the status quo and thus make people uncomfortable. A love-based psychology takes advantage of such "dis-ease" to gain important knowledge about people's needs and desires that could be seeds of their transformation, leading to new life directions and growth. Or, as Jungian analyst James Hillman put it, psychology with this perspective looks for "truths in errors in which deeper, more central necessities lie."[2]

By contrast, mainstream psychology, guided by the principle that people should be reasonable in their thinking and harmonious in their relationships, often functions like a massive defense system constructed to protect people from the very experiences that have the power to heal them. Instead of being open to the potential for change pregnant in people's difficulties, it seeks to help people assert control over themselves so they can return to their prior state of "normalcy," often involving repression and, later, destabilization. But the more logical and correct mainstream psychology tries to be, the worse its outcomes, or as Hillman said in his critique of psychology, "the righter it becomes, the wronger its effects."[3]

Principle 3: **A love-based psychology deals with the powers behind difficulties or disturbances as allies instead of enemies.**

When we go to sleep at night, we are often confronted by powerful forces over which we have limited control. We might dream of being attacked by lions, threatened by storms, or watching helplessly as others perform horrendous or miraculous deeds. We often appear small and impotent relative to these powers, and indeed we are. These are the same powers that fuel our most intractable difficulties, making them so hard to cope with. In treating these powers as allies, with which to engage, dance, or fight until we learn to relate to them, a love-based psychology helps us find ways to harness them to renew and enrich our lives.

By contrast, mainstream psychology disavows the powers that fuel difficulties, treating them as if our capacity to reason and take control over our lives is tantamount to the task of righting a ship. In this way, people's capacity to reason and take control over their lives is almost always used simply to return people to their former status quo—frequently a rigid condition that the difficulties surfaced to correct. Suggestions such as "Just say no," "Don't be unreasonable," "What were you thinking?" are usually ineffective in helping people deal with their greater difficulties, leaving them feeling powerless and ashamed of their inability to change. The failure of mainstream psychology programs to change people's habits, everything from addictions to eating patterns, testifies to the limitation of this approach.

Principle 4: **A love-based psychology treats the difficulties individuals and groups have as their own but also belonging to the greater web of relationships and culture.**

A love-based psychology views people's difficulties by taking into account the fact that they live in a web of relationships, including family, friendships, organizations, subcultures, and cultures. As Martin Luther King Jr. wrote, "We are caught in an escapable network of mutuality, tied in a single garment of destiny."[4] Accordingly, people's difficulties are seen not only as expressions of their own natures and struggles but also as expressions of other people's and groups' natures and struggles so that relationships, groups, and cultures bear some responsibility for the predicaments of individuals. From this perspective, treating people may take the form of individual counseling as well as broader-based interventions designed to change families, friendships, or the larger culture.

By contrast, mainstream psychology focuses its efforts mostly on individuals, treating, for example, people who lie, judge, fail to achieve, abuse substances, or abuse others, as if their personal weaknesses and pathologies alone are responsible for their difficulties.

Principle 5: **A love-based psychology treats individual and group diversity as natural and as expressive of wholeness and wellness.**

Just as nature's diversity is undeniable and ever emerging, the diversity of individuals, groups, and cultures is clearly evident. A love-based psychology is deeply democratic, appreciating and supporting individual and collective diversity in service of the natural beauty, power, and intelligence that informs it.

By contrast, mainstream psychology is guided by a powerful predisposition to help people live within their personal and the collective's narrow comfort zone. As a result, people's diversity is often seen as pathological instead of evidence of wholeness and beauty.

Principle 6: **A love-based psychology views social prejudice as impacting people's well-being, and the promotion of social justice as an important psychological intervention.**

Sexism, homophobia, classism, ethnocentrism, racism, and other forms of social bias play an integral role in the suffering people experience. Women's feelings about their bodies, black youths' success in the public education system, gay youths' experiences of prejudice or suicidal tendencies, and men's freedom to express vulnerability reflect the dominant culture's values and systems of control. Accordingly, a love-based psychology treats efforts to promote social justice as within the scope of psychology. As Cornel West, quoting Dr. Martin Luther King Jr., said, "Justice is what love looks like in public."[5]

By contrast, mainstream psychology often treats the difficulties of individuals in a vacuum, maintaining boundaries between social action and psychological intervention.

Principle 7: **A love-based psychology takes into account the fact that people's emotions and behavior are affected by how they are observed by others.**

Just as modern physicists have demonstrated that observers affect the behavior of even the smallest particles, modern psychology has also shown that people's behavior is influenced by the way they are observed. A love-based psychology asserts that people's behavior and feelings are affected by the way others view them and acknowledges that the relationship between change agents, such as counselors, and the people they seek to change impacts the efforts at transformation.

By contrast, mainstream psychology operates as if diagnoses are made through objective observation and the effectiveness of treatments is relatively independent of change agents or culture. It fails to see that the attitudes of change agents can fundamentally alter the feelings and behavior of people they seek to change, ignoring the relationship these agents have with the people under observation. For example, a woman urged to lose weight by a doctor might be so shamed that she either eats to comfort herself or starves herself to avoid judgment; a boy told he must stop lying by an angry parent might try to hide the truth of his actions and feelings to avoid punishment; and a man given drugs to enable sexual performance might turn against his tenderness, making him less capable of intimacy. Further, while the same principle is true when trying on their own to change aspects of themselves, people are often not conscious of the impact their critical attitudes have on their efforts.

In promoting dialogue about the role and practice of psychology in today's society, *Talking Back to Dr. Phil* uses issues raised in various episodes of the *Dr. Phil* show, including Dr. Phil's counsel about them. The *Dr. Phil* show is a prime example of the practice of mainstream psychology. Not only do his guests focus on problems to which many people in society can relate, but Dr. Phil regularly uses the lay audience's reactions as a litmus test for guests' psychological health and advises guests based on the perspective of mainstream psychology. Moreover, while examples of the practice of mainstream psychology abound, Dr. Phil, whose star rose like helium on the current of Oprah's repeated endorsements, is perhaps its most visible representative, considering that millions of people watch the *Dr. Phil* show daily on TV; read his best-selling books about weight loss, relationships, and family improvement; view his interviews with celebrities, presidents, movie stars, and rock musicians; and are aware of his role as spokesman for Match.com. Yet to date there are no books reflecting on his counsel, critiquing his approach, or providing alternatives to his advice. Thus the *Dr. Phil* show offers a familiar focal point for this analysis and critique of mainstream psychology and comparisons of it with the alternative approach to understanding emotions and behaviors that I call a love-based psychology.

Talking Back to Dr. Phil does not aspire to be neutral. Discussions of issues in it reflect the democratic attitude that informs my love-based psychology. Like the US Constitution, I do not adhere to majoritarianism, but rather protect marginalized people and forms of expression from being seen as "problems" and subjected to the shame of psychological labeling and cultural prejudice, and I explore people's difficulties to seek the seeds of their positive transformation.

Thus, for example, in the essays of this book:

- I defend large-bodied people from shame and criticism and look at the causes of their weight gain before I consider ways they can be helped to attain a weight that is healthier and more acceptable.
- I defend the meaningfulness of addicts' habits and attempt to understand them before I consider efforts to help them stop using substances.
- I defend the authority of women and explore its meaning for them rather than assume they need to be more accommodating or sensitive.
- I defend black youths' interest in sports and its significance in their lives before I consider how they can focus more on academics.
- I defend middle-aged women exploring their sexuality and consider its meaning for their lives before I assume that their sexual practices need to be more appropriate to accommodate those around them.
- I defend children's lying and attempt to understand its function before I try to help them tell the truth.
- I defend people who are judgmental and consider the reasons for this behavior, especially if they don't have the power to exercise authority, before I find ways to make their behavior more acceptable to others.

- I defend men who are tired of or resist being breadwinners and explore the meaning of this role in their lives before I encourage them to be more responsible.
- I address domestic violence by considering not only the roles of perpetrators and victims but also the role of the culture supporting it, realizing that our culture often practices an insidious denial of pain and teaches people to hide their suffering.

It is my hope that the insights presented in *Talking Back to Dr. Phil* will foster in readers a greater capacity to believe in themselves, especially in their most distressing and self-critical moments, as well as offer a new model for understanding themselves and others so that their personal problems are not viewed as indicators of inadequacy but rather indicators of the need for respect, compassion, and transformation.

PART I

Labeling, Lies, Judgment, and Anger

Call Me Crazy

Is Psychology Making Us Sick?

The world has such incredible variety;
why not join it, be that different thing, that other expression,
since that is what you are anyway, and love it?
—Alice Walker

WESTERN MEDICINE is based on an allopathic paradigm that includes three fundamental assumptions. First, deviations from the norm are manifestations of an underlying pathology. Second, treatment should eliminate or reduce symptoms of the underlying pathology. And third, health is equivalent to restoration of the prior norm.

For example, when we don't feel well we go to our doctor, who takes our temperature, orders blood tests, listens to our heart and lungs, and compares the resulting information to a norm based on thousands of other people. If our measurements fall within a certain range of that norm, we are considered normal, healthy. But if our measurements deviate too far from that norm we are deemed abnormal, unhealthy, and the doctor suggests treatment designed to bring our measurements back to normal and restore our health.

Mainstream psychology is also based on this allopathic paradigm. If people's behavior or experiences are too far from the norm, they are considered deviant or "sick." Subsequently, treatment is recommended to modify their behavior, normalizing them and making them healthy. I call diagnosing deviations from the norm as manifestations of an underlying pathology "allopathic thinking."

Allopathic thinking pervades our lives; it governs the way we treat ourselves, our friends, family members, coworkers, and people we don't know. For example, let's say I am normally a diligent, hardworking person trying to complete my first book, but I am spending significant time surfing the Internet, watching television, and chatting with friends. These behaviors are outside my norm, and I begin thinking, "What's wrong with me? Why aren't I working on my manuscript?" My "inner therapist" says, "You have a procrastination problem; reduce distractions, focus, and you will again be your normal diligent, hardworking self." If this doesn't work, I might read some self-help books, meditate, or go to my therapist to help me return to my usual ways. However, my disturbing behaviors may, in fact, represent an intelligent resistance to the way I usually approach my writing, reflecting that I could use a break, am too perfectionistic, or need some fresh ideas and perspectives.

To use another example, suppose my wife, usually a warmhearted person and great listener, starts behaving in a distant or irritable manner. I automatically think, "What's wrong with her? Isn't she getting enough sleep? Is there too much stress in her life?" After trying to diagnose the problem, I recommend treatment that will restore her and our relationship to their usual state. However, her disturbing behavior may instead represent an intelligent resistance to her normally more accommodating style, perhaps reflecting the fact that she has some deeper needs that are not being addressed. Whenever a person's behavior or experiences deviate from accepted norms, we employ the same paradigm, readily assuming something is wrong with them and making armchair diagnoses and treatment plans.

Such allopathic thinking is often fallacious for several reasons. First, just because people's behavior differs from the norm does not mean something is wrong with them. Their odd behavior could be a sign of healthy change if the norm according to which they have lived is too restrictive or oppressive. Or their idiosyncratic behavior might be a sign of genius rather than pathology. In short, allopathic thinking can "make people sick" for expressing their individuality or growth potential.

Second, allopathic thinking can be fallacious because we readily rely on our personal norms to make determinations about other people's behavior. When people behave in ways that deviate from our personal norms, we are likely to attribute their disturbing behavior to a pathology, thinking of them as "sick" and in need of treatment. We do this without considering that our personal norms have more to do with our own comfort levels, culture, and biases than any underlying pathology; without understanding the behavior that made us uncomfortable; and without critical examination of our intolerance of diversity. In effect, we often "make people sick" simply because they make us uncomfortable.

Third, allopathic thinking can be fallacious because we rely not only on personal norms but on the dominant culture's norms to determine whether people's behavior is pathological. This fallacy leads to questionable assessments about whole groups of people whose behaviors differ from those of the dominant culture. There is perhaps no better example of this fallacy than when homosexuality became condemned not only in the sphere of religion and morality but also in psychology, turning what was considered a sin by the dominant culture into a pathology. While there was no scientific basis for regarding homosexuality as a disorder, homosexuals were nonetheless diagnosed as sick. This dynamic is also used by governments intent on controlling various social or political groups. For example, a November 12, 2010 article by Sharon LaFraniere in the *New York Times* entitled "Assertive Chinese Held in Mental Wards" told the story of how people who sought redress from the Chinese government were regularly diagnosed with mental illness and hospitalized. It quoted Sun Dongdong, a forensic psychiatrist, as saying, "I have no doubt that at least 99 percent of China's pigheaded, persistent 'professional petitioners' are mentally ill."[1] In other words, the culture "made them sick."

These and other forms of allopathic thinking result in labeling and treating "disturbing" people or groups as sick in order to relegate them to the margins of society, dismiss their concerns, constrain their development, or coerce them to feel and act in more acceptable ways. I call this dynamic "pathologizing" people.

Our predisposition to restore a sense of normalcy as soon as possible when we feel disturbed or threatened by people's behavior leads us to pathologize individuals compulsively, insulating us from listening to their needs and desires, seeing their beauty and intelligence, and heeding their wisdom. As a result, we attribute disturbing qualities of others to pathologies and "treat" these qualities by trying to suppress them or fix them. This diminishes their value and functions as an insidious form of intolerance to diversity, whether expressed by an individual, group, or culture.

THE *DR. PHIL* SHOW

An episode of the *Dr. Phil* show provided good examples of how deviation from normal behavior is considered pathological.[2] The guests were a married couple dealing with the husband's long-term serious illness, which had required him to have a liver transplant about a year before the show. The couple had faced chronic stress, prohibitively high medical bills, and accompanying lifestyle changes. For a long time, the wife had been supportive, making the usual sacrifices: spending much of her time caring for her husband, working hard to pay high medical bills, adjusting her lifestyle, and worrying about her husband and their future. Eventually, however, she had grown increasingly resentful about the circumstances, protesting having to be so responsible for a condition she had not caused and objecting to the derailment of her dreams for the relationship and her own life, saying, "It's *his* illness. I didn't sign up for this."

Such feelings of resentment were not the norm for her. She, like most people in the culture, usually operated according to the ethic of sticking with someone "through thick and thin." As a result, she began to pathologize herself, thinking her resentment was caused by selfishness. She asked Dr. Phil if her feelings were normal in hopes that he would validate them as reasonable. Instead, Dr. Phil responded by defending the husband, telling her that his illness was not his fault as it was not due to alcohol abuse or any other bad habit for which he had failed to take responsibility. When the wife tried to support her position, saying there should be some limits to how much they spend on her husband's medical care, Dr. Phil retorted, "Isn't he worth it?" Dr. Phil then told her that her frustration and resentment were symptoms not only of her selfishness but of her "incredible insensitivity." In these ways, he let her know that her feelings were indefensible and the result of an underlying pathology. He communicated to the husband and the audience the idea that such feelings are unworthy of understanding and should be eliminated as if they were symptoms of an illness.

Next Dr. Phil intervened to rid the wife of her "illness." He chastised her and debated with her to show her the errors of her ways and to "cure" her by encouraging her to return to her more supportive behavior—a norm more acceptable to Dr. Phil and the dominant culture. Dr. Phil added power and punch to his message by enlisting the audience's support for this cure. He painted a picture for them of a man as an innocent victim not only of disease but also of his wife's insensitivity, never requiring the husband to defend himself. The audience applauded the manner in which Dr. Phil championed the husband and chastised the wife, creating an intervention that amounted to a public shaming—one of the most powerful ways to coerce people to change their behavior and turn them against themselves. Regrettably, Dr. Phil's perspective ignored the possibility that the husband, the nature of the couple's relationship, or the wife's legitimate needs had contributed to the wife's feelings or the tension between the couple.

NEW DIRECTIONS—PROCESS-ORIENTED PSYCHOLOGY

An alternative to the allopathic paradigm in psychology is process-oriented psychology, developed by Dr. Arnold Mindell in the mid-1970s. According to process-oriented psychology, when people's feelings or behaviors deviate from the norm it is considered a reflection of their individuality or their resistance to a norm that is too restrictive, oppressive, or otherwise no longer healthy. Thus their "symptoms" are indicative of an underlying urge toward health, wholeness, and diversity rather than pathology. And instead of treating symptoms by modifying or eliminating them, they are supported and amplified until their message becomes clear so the information gleaned from them can be used to enhance people's growth and the quality of their lives. Accordingly, health is not a state achieved when people are restored to a prior norm or level of acceptability to others but a process of development through which norms are evolving.[3]

Considering Dr. Phil's guests from this perspective can provide new insights into how their behavior might be evaluated. First, we would see the wife's growing "insensitivity" as a meaningful sign of her developing individuality. Before diagnosing her, we would take into account the fact that she had already spent considerable time and energy focusing on her husband's health and the subsequent financial difficulties; that her own needs and dreams had been put on hold in her efforts to be a sensitive caretaker; and that she probably had not had sufficient support for her feelings and stresses. While Dr. Phil, her husband, and the audience supported a return to her role as loving caretaker sacrificing for her sick husband, we would take her "insensitivity" as a sign of resistance to her prior role, and instead of treating her "insensitivity" by trying to eliminate it we would encourage her to get more support for herself and go even further in expressing her "insensitivity," leading her to perhaps state her needs more emphatically, saying, "Enough. It's time for my needs and difficulties to be addressed. It's time for me to be supported. It's time for sacrifices to be made for my health and dreams." Thus, becoming healthy would not mean returning to her prior norm but would involve becoming less focused on her husband's needs and more focused on her own. If she didn't do this, we would rightly expect her to become increasingly frustrated and resentful, any efforts toward making her more conforming to fail, and the couple's relationship to lose even more vitality and intimacy.

Next we would consider how the wife's "insensitivity" could be a healing force in her husband's life. Viewing it as meaningful, we would question the norm of treating her husband as if he were sick and in need of her sacrifices and sensitivity. We would contemplate whether his general well-being, perhaps even his physical health, would be better served by challenging him to assume more responsibility for his care and for the effect his illness was having on his marriage. Instead of thinking that the wife's statement "It's *his* illness" was insensitive, as Dr. Phil and the audience did, we would view her statement as containing a grain of truth. Through this lens, it becomes clear that the husband needs to take more ownership for the impact of his illness on the couple's lives and that a dose of "insensitivity" might be just what the doctor ordered.

Another example of this alternative approach is the case of Sassy, my wife Lisa's cat. Sassy had been taking medication for liver problems for about a year, but blood tests kept indicating that she was still not well.

Although the veterinarian said to continue giving her the medication and keep her indoors, Sassy began to resist the medication and paw at the door to be let out. In fact, she seemed to exhibit the most vitality when resisting her treatment. Thinking that her resistance was meaningful and not just something to overcome, like the wife's "insensitivity" on the *Dr. Phil* show, I crouched down alongside her and pulled gently on her leg and tail. She looked at me quizzically then meowed and pulled back. Going further with this tussling match, I could see she was showing more energy than she had for a long time. So Lisa and I decided to try a little experiment: take Sassy off the medicine for a while, let her out of the house, and repeat the blood test in a few months to monitor for change. Lo and behold, the test indicated significant improvement. Rather than enforcing the norm—the idea that Sassy was sick and required medicine—our approach of treating her resistance as meaningful and trusting that she would show us the direction of her healing resulted in aiding her recovery.

This kind of response to a long-term chronic illness is not as radical as it may seem. I have seen many people become disempowered by caretakers whose sympathetic and sensitive treatment of them ultimately entangled them in a relationship that might have looked compassionate but was actually making both people sick. I learned in my work at a Minnesota hospice that even the dying should be treated as if they can draw meaning and healing from their circumstances. In fact, diminishing returns have been noted when victims of disease are not treated as if they are capable and powerful.

The approach of process-oriented psychology might likewise be used to advantage with the couple on the *Dr. Phil* show. Dr. Phil supported the norm of their relationship, in which the wife was the sensitive care-taker who sacrificed her own needs and dreams for her husband's care. Thinking that the wife showing more sensitivity for the husband was the answer to their difficulties, Dr. Phil fought his battles for him, treating him as if he had not only a physical illness but emotional and relational weaknesses as well. A more productive approach for supporting the couple's relationship would be to require the husband to advocate for himself and the wife to address her challenges directly to her husband rather than to Dr. Phil. In this way, Dr. Phil would become a facilitator of their relationship rather than a moral arbiter taking the husband's side, and the couple would learn to communicate more directly with each other. Then perhaps the wife would give the husband the wake-up call he needs to take more ownership of his situation, and they could initiate a new level of honesty and intimacy in their relationship. Thus, according to this new paradigm the wife's "insensitivity" would not be interpreted as indicative of an illness to be cured but rather seen as reflecting a message that could reveal positive new developments for the wife, the husband, and their relationship. In this way, "insensitivity" would be the medicine, not the pathology.

Considering Dr. Phil's guests from the perspective of process-oriented psychology also sheds light on a critical fallacy that occurs when previously established norms set by the dominant culture for a particular subculture result in a member of that subculture being pathologized for feeling or acting outside the norm. The norms supported by Dr. Phil and amplified by his audience were those established by the dominant culture without consideration of their appropriateness for women. However, highlighting gender as a meaningful variable in understanding the wife's feelings turns our attention to the fact that she was in a role traditional for many women— that of caretaker sacrificing her own needs to make her husband's life the center of her universe—and gives us additional insight into her "insensitivity." From this perspective, being called "insensitive" might be the price she pays, as it is for many women resisting a traditional gender role, established as the norm by a patriarchal society, that is restrictive and oppressive. In this case, labeling her "insensitive" is less an accurate diagnosis and more an act of pathologizing her—dismissing her feelings and coercing her to conform to a norm for women that itself is in need of change. Seeing her "insensitivity" as meaningful, on the other hand, suggests a healing direction not only for her as a person but for her as a woman. From this perspective, rather than considering her sick for acting outside the culture's norm we would explore the possibility that it is not the wife who needs to be treated but the norms for women that need to be revised.

Treating the behavior of women who step outside society's normative gender role as pathological goes on all the time. For example, I remember the disdain students in my contracts class in law school had for a woman who spoke up as much as many vocal men. Since forcefulness and aggressiveness coming from a woman were outside the group's comfort zone, most of the students labeled the woman "competitive," "dominating," or "a real bitch" rather than seeing her behavior as a sign of her courage, intelligence, and passion. Consequently, they dismissed these qualities and tried to coerce her into acting in a manner that was acceptable and comfortable for them. Although students, both men and women, argued that she didn't need to be so aggressive to speak up (after all, the men didn't have the same tone and style), she was working against a culture that made it more difficult for her to do so (none of the other women spoke up as readily). While from the viewpoint of the established cultural norm this woman needed to become less aggressive and competitive, from another perspective her aggressiveness and competitiveness represented a healthy reaction to the cultural norm giving her just what she needed to make her voice heard. She didn't need to change; it was the rest of us who needed to become more tolerant of women like her and less tolerant of a gender-biased system.

Considering the role that gender plays in understanding the wife on the *Dr. Phil* show, while the husband might be a victim of her insensitivity to his needs, she might be a victim of the culture's insensitivity to her needs. From this perspective, she not only challenged the norm when she expressed insensitivity as a spouse, she also challenged the norm when she expressed insensitivity as a woman. The audience and both men on the stage, Dr. Phil and her husband, asserted that she was the one who needed to be more caring, but viewing the situation from a gender-aware perspective would suggest that it was actually Dr. Phil, her husband, and the audience who needed to change their notions about appropriate ways for a woman to express herself and behave in a relationship.

CONCLUSION

Whenever we or others act in a way that is outside the norm or that makes us uncomfortable, we, and mainstream psychology, tend to automatically think it indicates an underlying pathology in need of treatment. This is what the wife on the *Dr. Phil* show did when, disturbed by her own feelings, she asked Dr. Phil if they were normal. She looked to an authority, as many of us do, to either validate her feelings or affirm her diagnosis that she was not normal. Dr. Phil affirmed her diagnosis, dismissed her feelings, and coerced her to become more accommodating and acceptable as a person, as a spouse, and as a woman. In so doing, he taught her and her husband, along with millions of viewers, to diagnose and treat themselves and others similarly.

By contrast, process-oriented psychology resists assuming that people whose behavior departs from the norm have an underlying pathology. Instead, it teaches us to see such behavior as capable of enlightening us about their motivations and helping us view their development and individuality with respect and trust. It further teaches us to treat the unknown with curiosity, to nurture seeds of change, and to appreciate diversity in ourselves and others. While equating health with the norm can be helpful in making diagnoses and maintaining harmony, it can also turn psychology into the practice of norm enforcement, pathologizing ourselves and others to serve these ends. In short, psychology can "make us sick."

Cocreating Dishonesty

Sex, Lies, and Psychology

Castaneda lied to don Juan, bragging about his knowledge of plants in order to impress the old Indian with his intelligence. Don Juan immediately recognized the lie. What bothered him, though, was not the lie itself but Castaneda's attitude toward it. Castaneda had not taken his own story seriously. He had not taken responsibility for it; he did not believe his own lie.
—Arnold Mindell

MAINSTREAM PSYCHOLOGY'S primary focus on the problems of individuals ignores both how people cocreate relationship problems and how social systems play a role in what appear to be individuals' problems. Since individuals, not relationships or groups, are mainstream psychology's focus, a person's problems are seen to arise as a result solely of that person— for instance, because of their biochemical imbalances, emotional disturbances, ineffective coping mechanisms, or lack of discipline.

Even when it comes to relationships, mainstream psychology usually focuses on the roles individuals play in creating relationships instead of how both people cocreate problems in a relationship, as reflected by the many books counseling people on how to be loved or act loving; how to protect themselves from abuse or control; and how to think, feel, or act with others as if they are islands isolated from the dynamics of their relationships. There is also plenty of advice for parents about how to manage their children's behavior, sometimes suggesting extreme measures, without addressing the relationships between the parents and children, or the role parents play in cocreating children's behavior. In truth, the problems of

individuals are often cocreated by other people, either those in relationships with them or the social systems in which the individuals live. For example, while about 10 percent of school-aged boys are prescribed Ritalin
for learning and attention difficulties, insufficient attention has been given
to the role education systems play, or the dynamics of race and poverty, in
cocreating these difficulties.[1]

Mainstream psychology's focus on individuals as the culprit is perhaps
most pronounced with regard to lying—compulsive lying, pathological
lying, and habitual lying. Treatment methods for such individuals range
from medication and punishment to counseling and hypnosis. People in
relationships with liars are often viewed as victims rather than cocreators
of dishonesty. And systems within which lying flourishes, even in the presence of secrets, lack of transparency, and abuse of authority, are generally
deemed unaccountable for cocreating dishonesty. Typically, these systems,
like the Catholic Church with regard to sexual abuse scandals, are only
held accountable to the extent that they fail to identify and prosecute the
individuals who lie.

THE *DR. PHIL* SHOW

An episode of the *Dr. Phil* show provided good examples of how
mainstream psychology treats lying as a problem created by individuals
rather than cocreated by numerous individuals or social systems.[2] On the
show, a husband told about how he had watched pornography and lied
to his wife about it. Being of Christian faith, as was his wife, he went
to his church to get counseling for his habit. Dr. Phil focused not on
the husband's motivation for being interested in pornography but rather
on the man's lying, telling him he needed to become more self-confident
so that he could be more honest. He considered the man's lying to be a
greater violation of the marriage than watching pornography. Dr. Phil

also challenged the wife for being more focused on the pornography than on what he considered the core violation, the lying. He told her not to be deluded, that a man who watched pornography *and lied about it* could not be trusted. The audience readily aligned themselves with Dr. Phil's attitude, eclipsing further understanding of the husband or consideration of the wife's role in the dishonesty.

Thus, Dr. Phil treated the man as if he were the liar and the woman as if she were the victim of his lying. However, Dr. Phil never explored the extent to which the relationship itself may have been dishonest, especially regarding issues of sexuality.

Nor did he consider the role that social systems, especially the church, played in the husband's dishonesty about pornography. Neglecting the social context conveys a message that individuals rather than systems need to be held accountable, reinforcing blindness to the social contexts that cocreate the problems of individuals and thus dismissing our collective responsibility for such problems.

Finally, Dr. Phil never delved into the issues of pornography or sexuality. He suggested that a lie is a lie regardless of content. Like mainstream psychology, he confined his analysis to the moral breach—lying is bad and should be corrected. Going beyond the moral breach is not typically seen as necessary or useful. However, it is my viewpoint that deeper understanding of the underlying dynamics that fuel individual and group behavior ought to be the province and responsibility of psychology.

THE COMPLICITY OF OTHERS IN DISHONESTY

Clearly there was some truth to the view expressed by Dr. Phil that the man's lying perpetrated a violation against his wife and that she was victimized by his dishonesty. However, this might not have been the whole truth. According to my experience working with couples, it is likely that she might also have been dishonest with him in some way, and both of them may bear some culpability for the dishonesty in their relationship, particularly related to their sexuality.

Consider, for example, the case of a colleague of mine who at age ten was confronted by his father about cheating on a test. The day before the confrontation, his father had received a call from the son's math teacher, who had relayed evidence of his son's cheating. The father asked his son, "Did you cheat on your math test?" The father's tone was fierce; I imagined fear in the boy's eyes as if the police in some totalitarian state were interrogating him. Quickly the word *no* fell from the scared boy's lips. That was all the father needed to hear; he concluded that his son was not only a cheater but, worse, a liar. He presented the evidence to his son and announced his punishment.

The father believed that the son needed to be taught a lesson about respecting his parents and being an honest person. But as a therapist I wanted to know more about the boy's motivations and the role the father had played in the scenario. Why didn't the son tell his father the truth? What was his relationship with his father like? And why didn't the father tell the truth—that he knew he cheated—instead of setting up another test?

As I gained more information, it became evident that the son was under extreme pressure from his father to do well in school, had often been afraid of his father, and had little interaction with him when the father was not acting as evaluator or enforcer. The father was an angry, vengeful man who actually enjoyed exposing people who lied to him or betrayed him. Although the son had lied, the father also bore some responsibility for creating a relationship built on fear and mistrust. And, in a way, the father was also dishonest, questioning his son as if he didn't know the son had cheated. If the father had created a safer and more trusting relationship that fostered easier communication with his son, he might have discovered that his son's fear of disappointing him and need for his love had contributed to his cheating and lying. Looking at the context makes it likely that our outrage at the son's lying and cheating would be mitigated by our understanding and compassion for him. We might even feel some outrage toward the father since although the son disrespected the father the reverse was also true. They had cocreated a dishonest relationship.

While the above story is different from the story of the guests on the *Dr. Phil* show, they are similar in one essential way—Dr. Phil, like the father, focused on the individual who lied and not the context of the relationship. Paying attention to the dynamics between people and the social context can provide crucial information and an alternative perspective. For example, it could be informative to consider how the wife on the *Dr. Phil* show might not have been entirely honest about sexuality with her husband—perhaps she had been unable to tell the truth about her need for intimacy, the way she wanted to be touched, her fear of being touched, her feelings about her body, or about being attractive or unattractive. Perhaps she was terrified or disgusted by sexual intimacy and never admitted this to her husband or recoiled from his advances or avoided moments of sexual intimacy without explaining why. Perhaps both of them were ashamed of their sexuality and had not spoken honestly about their fears or personal history regarding sexuality. If any of these dynamics occurred in the relationship, it could change our perspective about the husband's lying and the wife's part in the circumstances as it occurred with the father and son. We would then spend more time focusing on the details of his *and* her feelings, needs, and experiences around sexuality to help this couple communicate better about their sexuality. Thus more information about the context of situations can be important for our understanding and the type of interventions indicated for treatment.

Certainly we should not seek to blame the victim, in this case the wife, especially in a culture whose patriarchal prejudices and trespasses are already too easily dismissed. But we do need to realize that when it comes to healing relationships psychology too easily finds one person to blame for a dynamic that both people have cocreated and which can only be healed by both.

THE COMPLICITY OF SOCIAL SYSTEMS IN DISHONESTY

When exploring the context of individuals' problems, it also becomes evident that social systems often cocreate these problems. We know that the husband on the *Dr. Phil* show went to his church for counseling about his viewing of pornography. While the counsel the husband got from his church was not discussed on the show, I have spoken with several men who have been counseled by their ministers after being caught viewing pornography. In none of these situations was there acknowledgment of the role the church as a social system played in these men's behavior or dishonesty. Understanding the men's motivations to view pornography, and the role the church played in it, was not part of the healing equation.

However, it is known that social systems play a critical role in human behavior. One of the groundbreaking research projects demonstrating this truth was conducted in 1971 at Stanford University by Philip Zimbardo. Zimbardo simulated a prison with student volunteers who were randomly chosen to play the role of either prisoner or prison guard. Zimbardo found that students who played the role of guard became cruel and authoritarian, while those who played the role of prisoner became rebellious, angry, and depressed. The assigned roles had such a powerful impact on the students that the two-week study had to be terminated after six days because of the traumatizing effect it was having.[3] While most people attribute experiences such as rebelliousness, anger, and depression to individuals, Zimbardo showed that social conditions, in a matter of days, had the power to transform normal people into immoral, traumatized, and pathological individuals. With this in mind, it might be revealing to discover whether the church to which Dr. Phil's guests belonged played a role, as a social system, in the husband's behavior and dishonesty, perhaps operating, with regard to sexuality, as a kind of criminal justice system analogous to the prison system Zimbardo simulated.

Consider the case of a man I counseled who hid his interest in pornography from his family and church, realizing that if it came to light their condemnation would be severe. He would have to leave the church and his wife for at least several months then go through an "oral examination" by the elders to prove he had changed before being allowed back into the life of his family or community. Interestingly, his family and church had offered only one teaching about sex as he had grown up—any form of sexuality was wrong and sinful except within marriage and any sexual exploration was cause for shame and punishment. Consequently, from an early age he had learned to hide his sexual impulses and refrain from seeking guidance from his family or community.

The man lied about viewing pornography, but this was not the whole truth. After living in a social system that fostered secrecy and suppression his whole life, he had internalized those messages and was now suppressive, condemning, and effective at keeping his underlying needs secret, even from himself. Helping this man become more honest with himself and others required encouraging him to defend himself against his shaming, punishing, and repressive family and church. Before he could begin to explore his sexual feelings, needs, and desires, he had to see how his family and church had played a formative role in his inability to be honest with himself and others. This might also be true for the husband on the *Dr. Phil* show even though Dr. Phil treated him as an individual independent of his family and church, as if they were not implicated in his behavior. In a way, Dr. Phil became a kind of agent of the church, a moral authority expressing the same punishing indignation that may have contributed to the man's lack of honesty, while avoiding deeper exploration of the husband's motivations for being interested in pornography and his inability to be honest about his needs and feelings that could have shed more light on the psychological dynamics of the situation.

The way any social system achieves its ends, whether through love and understanding or punishment and repression, has a powerful impact on people's ability to be honest with themselves and others. Sometimes its approach can make expressions of forbidden impulses more deviant. We are all aware of the scandal in the Catholic Church regarding priests' sexual abuse of children, and we readily judge the priests and condemn the Church's complicity in covering up details and not taking swifter action to address cases of accused priests. But what is largely left unchallenged is how the Church's repressive and shaming attitude toward sexuality contributes to the deceitful and deviant manner in which sexuality is expressed by Church officials. When any social system forbids an aspect of human behavior, it is likely that behavior will be explored in the shadows, far from the light of reflection that can ensure people are not abused in the process.

In considering that the Church, or another repressive social system, could play a role in not only cocreating dishonesty about sexuality but also fostering deviant expressions of sexuality, I consulted a psychologist colleague of mine who has worked with sex offenders for more than twenty years. He told me that nations allowing freer and less guilt-inducing access to pornography, such as Scandinavian countries, Japan, and Spain, have much lower rates of sexual abuse, only 20 to 25 percent of that of the United States. He also said that some people will always be triggered by pornography, but for a more significant number it acts as a relief valve, allowing for fantasies rather than repressing them until they lead to behavior harmful to others. Lastly, he told me that the most difficult step in working with offenders was getting them to be honest with themselves about their impulses, desires, and interests.[4]

It seems evident that social systems play a significant role in individual behavior, including lying and sexual expression. Although from the perspective of mainstream psychology individuals are wholly responsible for themselves, from this larger perspective individuals and social systems cocreate problems, and the problems with one reflect problems with the other. While understanding this does not change individuals' responsibility, culpability, or need for help, it does expand our understanding of problems, making it more difficult for those who identify with social systems to throw stones without considering their own role in creating the problems of individuals.

BEYOND MAINSTREAM MORALITY: LOOKING BEHIND LIES

Mainstream psychology often considers immoral behavior, as defined by the mainstream culture, to be psychologically problematic if not pathological, and analysis stops when the problem has been identified. This cuts off further exploration of the meaning and purpose of the behavior. As such, psychology serves mainstream morality but neglects its calling to explore the depths of psyche and soul.

On the *Dr. Phil* show, Dr. Phil intervened to stop the husband from lying—a moral breach considered also to be a psychological problem—but did not explore his motivations for lying about viewing pornography. Other mainstream approaches, including church counseling, also limit interventions to stop a person from viewing pornography. In these and other investigations, psychology conducts a moral evaluation and determines a treatment in the form of reprimand, punishment, or shaming.

But honoring psychology's unique role of exploring and understanding the psyche requires further investigation and a deeper analysis. In the case of the husband on the *Dr. Phil* show, this would mean examining the underlying needs, fantasies, impulses, and desires that fuel this man's interest in pornography. People view pornography for a myriad of reasons. Some men who are intimidated by the pressure to sexually perform turn to pornography to find sexual pleasure without such pressure. If the husband revealed such a dynamic, then helping him stop viewing pornography would require assisting him with his sexual performance anxiety. Others view pornography to explore, or vicariously engage in, a particular type of sexual activity that they would be too ashamed to talk about with their partner. If this is the husband's situation, he and his wife would need to learn to talk to each other about their particular interests. Still other individuals view pornography because it allows them emotional or psychological freedom, permitting them to be vulnerable, strong, assertive, receptive, self-soothing, or playful in ways not possible in their relationship because of their own inhibitions or their partner's or culture's restrictions—or all three. If this is the case with the husband, becoming honest would require a new level of intimacy with his wife, to the point where they could share their fears, needs, and fantasies. This is in contrast to the perspective of mainstream psychology, which limits the notion of honesty to the husband telling his wife that he is viewing pornography.

CONCLUSION

Mainstream psychology too readily focuses only on individuals as the source of their problems, while deeper investigation reveals that both people in a relationship cocreate these problems as do social systems that foster fear, secrecy, repression, and shame. When rejection, shame, and criticism comes from a powerful force in our lives, such as our partnership, family, religious institution, place of employment, or community, many of us do not speak the truth. Almost everyone who has ever felt disempowered—as a child, student, employee, woman, person of color, or outsider—knows the urge to deceive or lie to protect themselves.

By contrast, alternative approaches in psychology that look beyond the individual toward relationships and social systems give us a more complete understanding of an individual's behavior by analyzing it in context. These alternative approaches also expand treatment options, suggesting interventions focused on relationships as well as interventions designed to impact dysfunctional social systems. In addition, they make our moral judgments against individuals relative, steering us away from scapegoating others and making it clearer how, in many ways, we all have a measure of responsibility for the problems in our world.

In the Shadow of Our Judgments
Ethics and Psychology

Everyone carries a shadow, and the less
it is embodied in the individual's conscious life,
the blacker and denser it is.
—C.G. Jung

MAINSTREAM PSYCHOLOGY treats judgmentalism as a demon, ignoring the riches that might be uncovered through deeper exploration. It considers judgmentalism to be a form of moral weakness resulting from our reactivity, lack of humility, or mean-spiritedness. In addition, it teaches that judgmentalism is often based on unverified assumptions. Internet and print articles, books, and therapists counsel us to overcome our judgmentalism to cure us of this error-producing and unseemly habit.[1]

Such an approach fails to account for the fact that we tend to judge those who offend our sensibilities—people who do things we never do or let ourselves do. Consequently, some people are particularly subject to our judgments, while others are not. For example, some people target democrats and some republicans. Some target hippies, while others target corporate executives. Some target drug addicts, while others target the straight laced. Mainstream psychology treats the targets of our judgments as irrelevant, however, focusing solely on the judgmentalism itself.

In addition, mainstream psychology does not adequately address why we cling to certain judgments and easily let go of others. It doesn't explain, for instance, why we may spend hours listening to talk radio shows and television shows that deride those we judge, adding fuel to our fire, and why we don't simply take the advice of the many articles, books, and therapists to rid ourselves of this limiting habit.

THE *DR. PHIL* SHOW

An episode of the *Dr. Phil* show provided good examples of how judgmentalism is often viewed by practitioners of mainstream psychology.[2] The guest, a woman from a small town, was married to a local preacher and appeared to live a conservative lifestyle. She complained of being too judgmental, a quality at odds with her personal and Christian ethic. She noted a particular tendency to judge people who rode motorcycles and had tattoos.

Dr. Phil found her habit of being judgmental somewhat offensive and saw it as a kind of prejudice based on false assumptions that needed to be eliminated. Consequently, he suggested a clever intervention, convincing his guest to spend a day with a "friend" of his—as it turned out, a man with long hair and tattoos who drove a Harley-Davidson. Dr. Phil arranged this meeting because he knew his "friend" was not at all what his guest expected and would expose her false assumptions and repudiate her prior judgments.

The intervention had the desired effect. Although the woman was at first aghast at seeing the tattooed biker at her door, she ended up having a great time with him, saying, "It was more fun than I want to admit." The man was kind and thoughtful, and not intimidating or irresponsible, as she had suspected tattooed bikers were. When the biker joined her on the show, the sparkle in her eyes reflected her upbeat energy, making it clear that she had become a more generous-spirited person less prejudiced against bikers with tattoos. However, the deeper meaning of her judgmentalism was never explored.

EXPLORING THE DEEPER MEANING OF JUDGMENTALISM

In contrast to mainstream psychology's approach to judgmentalism, depth psychology, including the various forms of Jungian psychology, provides a basis for a deeper understanding of it, more potent interventions, and a broader vision of moral development. According to this approach, the targets of our judgmentalism actually represent unacknowledged aspects of ourselves. The eminent Swiss psychiatrist Carl Jung said that each of us has qualities we find particularly objectionable or morally reprehensible. We are predisposed to deny these aspects of ourselves, or "split them off," much like when a drunken person says, "That's the alcohol talking; that's not really me." Together these split-off aspects form what Jung called the shadow—parts of ourselves hidden from our consciousness. Relegating aspects of ourselves to the shadow makes us strangers to parts of ourselves, like embodying a Dr. Jekyll and Mr. Hyde who are unaware of each other. It is as if our right hand doesn't know what our left hand is doing, making it nearly impossible to be responsible for our darker motives.

But while denying these qualities blinds us to their existence in ourselves, it makes us more inclined to see them in others. The more invested we are in denying the existence of these qualities, the denser and darker our shadow is and the more fuel we provide for our projections and judgments of others—whom we view as having the moral failings and inferiorities, in contrast to us. In its most vicious form, this dynamic dehumanizes others and subjects them to injustices, as has been the case with all vilifications of peoples throughout history.

The woman on the *Dr. Phil* show presented a classic case of projection. She didn't see herself to be similar, in any way, to people who rode motorcycles and had tattoos—they wouldn't drive the same car, live in the same house, speak as gently, or be married to the same kind of person. The woman denied possessing their qualities and the untapped powers they represented, and consequently projected these qualities onto other people, making them the targets of her judgment. Because Dr. Phil's mainstream approach to judgmentalism focused only on the habit of being judgmental, it failed to investigate why she had been judgmental about bikers with tattoos. Instead, she could have learned how claiming aspects of herself that reflected the qualities she saw in bikers with tattoos would empower her moral and spiritual development.

Depth psychology offers a useful means of understanding split-off qualities through exploring projections in dreams, recognizing that split-off qualities are projected not only onto people in our daily lives but also onto figures in our dreams, appearing, for example, as monsters, people victimizing us, animals we fear, or even forces of nature that threaten us such as storms or earthquakes.

The following dream illustrates this phenomenon. In the dream a man, apparently on a safari, is hunting a lion in the woods. He is on the lion's trail, evident from the dead and eaten prey he sees along his path. When he catches sight of the lion, it turns toward him. He becomes frightened and, unprepared to take on the lion, decides to retreat. The man who had this dream recalled seeing lions on television, in movies, and in zoos, especially one with an incredible roar at the opening of each MGM movie, but he didn't know what lions were really like—whether they attacked if individuals came upon them in the wild, how they communicated with one another, or how they fit into the web of life. He simply had a preconception that lions had three qualities, all of which are seen in the dream: powerful, frightening roars, a natural instinct to stalk their prey, and the capacity to kill. His preconception and limited knowledge about lions made them the perfect image on which to project his own shadow qualities as is reflected in the conversation we had and my subsequent interpretation of it:

I asked: What are you currently struggling with in your life?

He replied: I am afraid about my career. I want to leave my job as an account manager, which I have held for fifteen years. I have been thinking about making the change for a few years now, but the security of my current position is very compelling. I get right up to the edge of the decision and then back off. (*Interpretation*: The dream suggests that the lion can do what he cannot. He projects aspects of himself onto the lion. Just like he gets close to the lion then backs off, he gets close to leaving his job and changing his career then backs off; he doesn't want to acknowledge his potential predatory nature, power, and mastery. However, he will need to claim these qualities if he is going to resolve his career dilemma.)

I asked: What stops you from leaving your job?

He replied: Lots of people start their own companies; many of them get eaten alive. (*Interpretation*: This comment makes it clear that he also projects upon the marketplace. To him the marketplace, like a lion, is ruthless, self-serving, and can eat him alive.)

I asked: Do you know any people who have been successful at it?

He replied: Yes, two women I used to work with, the people who caused me to seriously think about setting out on my own.

I asked: What were they like?

He replied: When they first left the company, I thought they were irresponsible; I thought they should work on their startup on the side and not burn their bridges with the company until they knew it would be successful. But they seemed to use the company and connections to further their own agenda. You know, they were those cutthroat business-people who have little regard for others. (*Interpretation*: He also projected onto these women. They were like lions who took decisive actions and went after what they want-ed, shadow parts of himself he could not acknowledge. He needed to learn not only not to judge these women but to be like them.)

I asked: What would you do if you were like them, if you were irresponsible, a cutthroat businessman, willing to burn bridges?

He replied: I would just leave my job and do what I have been wanting to do for a long time. (*Interpretation*: If he could claim the qualities that he split off, he would not only be less judgmental of the women but more whole and better able to accomplish what he wanted in life.)

I asked: But what about your family? What if you don't make it?

He replied: If you don't go for what you want, you're kind of dead already. (*Interpretation*: He projected onto the business world, seeing it as a lion killing him, its prey. While logi-cally the answer might be to find a place safe from the lion, psychologically the safest response is to become a lion. He needed to stop projecting onto people and circumstances he judged and claim these aspects of the lion, his own split-off qualities.)

About six months after our conversation, the man left his job. Telling his employer he was leaving meant speaking up (roaring like a lion), put-ting an end to his old life ("killing" it), and stalking his new life. This man's denial of his capacity to make life-changing decisions had fueled his judgments, so he projected his split-off qualities onto two people, the women; an animal, the lion; and the marketplace. Simply working to rid this man of his judgmentalism while ignoring who his judgments targeted and what fueled them—denial and a real need to change his life—would not have empowered him to change for the better. To improve he actually needed to embrace the qualities he was judging.

Similarly, further exploring the judgmentalism of the woman on the *Dr. Phil* show through the lens of depth psychology could open the door to a powerful new path of moral development. Her current path, the one supported by Dr. Phil and much of mainstream psychology, simply teaches her to become a less judgmental person. However, understanding her projections has the power to alter her consciousness in several important ways.

First, to the extent the woman remains unaware of qualities she shares with tattooed bikers she will remain unaccountable for their emergence and subsequent consequences. When she acts out of character, she will be prone to think, "That wasn't me," or "I don't know what got into me," or "I'm sorry, I'm sure it won't happen again"—phrases fueled by denial. By contrast, claiming and integrating these qualities would allow her to be more honest with herself and others.

Second, recognizing that she actually shares the qualities she judges in the bikers with tattoos would help the woman empathize with such people and give her insights into a path for her own moral growth. Simply trying to avoid judging people, while morally noble, rarely puts an end to the sense of superiority inherent in judgment, resulting in pity or condescension toward the ones judged. This attitude can be detected, for example, in comments such as "It is not my place to judge you" or "I can't judge you, but . . . ," which can easily be interpreted as put-downs. By contrast, seeing how the qualities we judge in others are actually our split-off qualities leads to empathy with the targets of our judgmentalism and provides insights into the self. Accordingly, if the woman on the *Dr. Phil* show were to have such insights, she would likely treat tattooed bikers with an empathy that fosters relationship and a realization of the interconnectedness of all people, a moral goal of many spiritual traditions.

Ultimately, exploring judgmentalism would lead to comprehending the power that shadow and projection have on societal campaigns to marginalize and dehumanize entire groups of people from indigenous nations, women, and people of color to the mentally ill, the poor, and even children. The inclination to vilify groups of people is among the greatest moral challenges worldwide, and understanding how denial creates shadow and leads to projection antidotes this tendency. It encourages people to turn their attention from their targets to their own blindness, confronting them with the wisdom of Walt Kelly's cartoon character Pogo, who memorably said, "We have met the enemy, and they are us."

To use depth psychology's methods to better help Dr. Phil's guest with her judgmentalism, we would need to know more about her projections onto tattooed bikers, whom she sees as irresponsible and intimidating. Perhaps her projections recapitulate the culture's stereotypical views of bikers with tattoos.[3] These can reflect aspects not only of the shadow of individuals but also the shadow of the culture in general. It is as if the whole culture "dreams" of tattooed motorcycle riders.

Considering the following three cultural stereotypes and what they might say about Dr. Phil's guest can help us better understand the motivations behind her judgmentalism and how projections work in both individuals and society.

The Outcast Rebel. A major cultural stereotype portrays bikers as outcast rebels. Perhaps the best expression of this image is presented in the counterculture film *Easy Rider*, which tells the story of two freewheeling hippy bikers who break free from mainstream material life, making the open road their home and adventure their destination. Armed with this information, we could perhaps help Dr. Phil's guest with her judgmentalism by encouraging her to integrate these qualities. We could begin by having her consider how she might be an outcast rebel herself in some way but denies this aspect of herself. Interestingly, she said that when she was with the tattooed biker she had "more fun than I want to admit." While she might work hard to act conventionally, some part of her may desire to break free of that role, be more adventurous, and express her individuality. We could then work with her to explore the directions in which this freedom might take her, including, perhaps, vocations outside the family or church or new ways of enjoying life. We could also address the possibility that integrating her "outcast rebel" would be made more difficult by the fact that she and members of her community might view the qualities she shares with the outcast rebel—such as a sense of rebellion or disregard for the rules and norms of society—as irresponsible. Subsequently, we could also help her deal with this challenge.

The Tough Guy. Another cultural stereotype about bikers with tattoos is that they are tough guys—military men, sailors, criminals, or thugs. See Georgia Hackworth's "Stigmas, Stereotypes of Tattooing"[3] and "Skin Stories,"[4] aired on Public Broadcasting Service, for additional exploration of this image.

With such information in mind, we could perhaps help Dr. Phil's guest by having her explore what it means for her to be tougher—for example, speaking more directly about her beliefs or standing up to certain people. This kind of exploration might enable her to relate more authentically to people in her community with whom she disagrees; give her the ability to speak out against injustices; or make it possible for her to take on roles she feels are beyond her capacity.

We could also address the possibility that integrating her toughness could be made more difficult because she and members of her community likely view such toughness as too intimidating and unrefined, or not sufficiently soft or feminine. Then we could also help her deal with this challenge.

The Biker Chic. A third cultural stereotype of bikers with tattoos is the biker chic. This image carries with it the impression of being an outlaw and tough, but it also connotes outward self-expression, especially sexual expression. For example, Ashley Ford, in her article "Tattoo Stereotypes,"[5] and M. M. Rooni, in his article "Body Art—Tattoo Stereotypes,"[6] write about how women with tattoos are often seen as having sexually "loose morals," and a common tattoo for women, displayed on the lower back, is referred to as the "tramp stamp."

Claiming her "inner biker chic" might give Dr. Phil's guest access to the capacity to express herself more courageously, powerfully, and radically. Her self-expression might take the form of flaunting an artistic hairstyle, proclaiming her views more publicly, enjoying her body through sensual pleasures, or appreciating her beauty more openly through dressing in less restricted ways that make her feel good. Because the patriarchal culture has used women's bodies and sexuality as a lever in curtailing their power, claiming her "inner biker chic" might, in fact, provide her with a profound sense of empowerment as a woman rather than making her feel unfeminine.

We could also address the possibility that claiming this kind of self-expression could be made more difficult by the fact that she and her community would likely view such expression as offensive or unladylike. Subsequently, we could also help her deal with this challenge.

Considering these cultural stereotypes to be similar to the qualities Dr. Phil's guest is projecting onto bikers with tattoos gives us a window on how she might combat her judgmentalism by looking at herself, integrating split-off qualities, and addressing new challenges. She might become not only a "nicer," less judgmental person but also more authentic, empowered, and courageous.

In addition, encouraging her to understand and integrate such split-off qualities as opposed to simply trying to stop her from being judgmental, might enrich her spiritual life in numerous ways. It might help her connect with people in her community who feel like outcasts, from people who have addictions or act outside the law to those with marginalized sexual orientations or who practice a different faith. It might also help her listen empathetically to those who speak up against her community or church practices. On a spiritual level, it might help her see others as not separate from herself. However, if she does not integrate these qualities, she will relegate them to her shadow, rendering her unable to take responsibility for these aspects of herself and making it likely that she will continue to vilify bikers with tattoos, or some other suitable target, and limit her capacity to genuinely connect with people who express their qualities.

CONCLUSION

Although becoming less judgmental is a morally worthy goal, mainstream psychology's efforts to simply banish our demons, including the demon of judgmentalism, can leave us less aware of ourselves and less able to use our full potential. The renowned twentieth-century German poet Rainer Maria Rilke intimated this when his friend Lou Andreas-Salomé, acutely aware of Rilke's psychic struggles, offered to secure him a course of psychoanalysis with Sigmund Freud, with whom she had trained, and he replied that he feared in eliminating his demons he might lose his angels as well.[7]

The approach of depth psychology, on the other hand, can help augment our potential and enrich our lives. From this perspective, we understand that our judgments are fueled by our own split-off qualities relegated to our shadows and projected onto others, marginalizing or demonizing them, and we learn to explore our shadows and claim these split-off aspects of ourselves to become more empowered and whole, gain a broader perspective on life, and achieve enlightenment about the commonalities among all people.

Anger

Befriending the Beast

To suppress or take away our anger
is to suppress or take away ourselves.
—Thich Nhat Hanh

WE NEED TO BE CAREFUL when we come upon a wild beast. Knowing it can overpower us, we rightly fear its capacity to injure us. Out of concern for our safety, we might be inclined to run away, cage it, anesthetize it, or even kill it. Few choose to meet the animal on its own terms to study its true nature, power, and motivations. We respond to anger similarly, fearing it can make us feel small and act destructively. To avoid letting it overtake us or to modulate its power, we tell ourselves it's not good to be angry; we count to ten, bite our lip, and swallow what sometimes can be a bitter pill.

Various spiritual traditions, from Buddhism to Judaism and Christianity, also seem to counsel against anger. The Buddha likened being angry to grabbing a hot ember—the longer we hold on, the more we get burned. The Jewish tradition suggests a process of atonement that relieves us of the anger separating us from others. The Christian faith counsels us to turn the other cheek and forgive.

Mainstream psychology advocates a similar orientation to anger, focusing on eliminating or managing it. In books, workshops, and therapy sessions, we are taught to take time-outs, forgive, let go, not take things personally, or, if necessary, express our anger in a controlled situation to release it. Whether we are counseled to calm down or scream out loud, elimination or management of anger is the goal. While this orientation may make us temporarily safer, it causes suppression of anger, making it likely the anger will manifest only in ways that are less expected or recognizable.

By contrast, looking at anger as a wild beast that we need to befriend rather than treat as an enemy, can help us better understand its characteristics, our relationship to it, and its power to sabotage relationships and disrupt our lives. Psychology can help us build a relationship with anger that will leave us more aware of its message and better able to integrate its power to transform its energy for a healthier life.

THE *DR. PHIL* SHOW

An episode of the *Dr. Phil* show provided good examples of how people suppress their anger, the dangerous consequences, and mainstream psychology's approach to anger.[1] This episode focused on members of a family who had lived a life poisoned by the anger that arose after a tragic accident. Fifteen years earlier, a woman named Gretchen had been the driver of a car involved in an accident that left her sister, a passenger in the car, partially paralyzed. Gretchen suffered from debilitating guilt, while her sister suffered from chronic anger that clouded her vision and crippled her relationships. Their father was furious at Gretchen, and their mother naively tried to make the family's pain and anger go away without actually addressing it. None of the family members had talked about the accident or expressed their feelings but instead had suppressed their anger, each in different ways, hoping it would dissipate. However, their suppressed anger had simply manifested in less recognizable ways.

Gretchen's suppressed anger had manifested in a common manner—as internalized guilt. Instead of expressing her anger directly by talking to her sister about what an awful thing she had done and how unfair the accident's effects on her sister had been, she buried her feelings in guilt, experiencing nightmares and emotional trauma every day. Her distorted sense of responsibility had caused her to spend fifteen years seeking doctors who might heal her sister's injury. In addition, she had punished herself, refusing to do things she loved, including acting and singing. Her suppressed anger acted like a sniper, attacking her with blame, forcing her to spend her time trying to fix what she could no longer control, and sabotaging all her possibilities for joy and fulfillment.

Her sister's anger had manifested in another form—chronic resentment that had lasted the fifteen years since the accident. While she tried to keep her resentment under wraps, it nonetheless made it difficult for her to make friends, although she explained this difficulty away by saying that people didn't understand her. Her suppressed anger acted like a toxic atmosphere, coloring her moods; poisoning her relationships, especially with her sister; and sapping her life force.

Their father's suppressed anger had manifested in yet another way—forgiving and accommodating behaviors for periods of time, then unexpected explosions. While he might have given the impression of being at peace, his anger would suddenly erupt in dangerous and hurtful ways. Suppressed, his anger acted like a terrorist, disguising itself in the garb of reasonableness and acceptance while planting bombs and unexpectedly detonating them. For example, at one point he took Gretchen for a ride in his car, deliberately speeding up to one hundred miles per hour and saying, "See what it feels like?"

People who erupt in such ways are commonly described as having "bad tempers." Characteristically, they blow up, apologize, and then re-establish their equilibrium without ever exploring or directly expressing their underlying anger. Individuals who have bad tempers, which are like pressure cookers with very tight lids that can get blown off, typically do not "let off steam" by expressing their anger in controlled ways but instead allow pressure to build to the point where they "flip their lids." While mainstream psychology usually sees anger as the source of such behavior, this dynamic has as much to do with suppression.

Gretchen's mother's suppressed anger had manifested in yet a fourth way—through attempts to control everyone's pain and establish harmony. But although she said she wanted to make peace in the family she acted in ways that were ineffectual. For instance, as part of her effort to control the sisters' anger after their father's death she insisted that he had forgiven everyone before dying, which, was found to be untrue. The mother had been willing to twist the truth to avoid conflict. Her attempts to put a lid on the expression of difficult feelings among family members actually perpetuated their forms of suppressed anger—internalized guilt, chronic resentment, and unexpected explosions.

Thus each family member on the *Dr. Phil* show found a strategy to suppress anger and manifest it in a less recognizable but more insidious form. When we encounter such forms of suppressed anger, they seem simply destructive. However, experiencing manifestations of suppressed anger is not the same as meeting the underlying anger itself, the beast, and understanding its message and power.

For example, a client recently came to me for what he called a "drinking problem." I was surprised to learn he drank only once every couple of weeks, with his friends after work, but I quickly understood his difficulty when he told me his wife wanted him to get help because he was hostile and abusive after coming home on those nights. I said, "Oh, you have an anger problem," to which he replied, "No, I have a drinking problem. I only get angry when I drink." He not only resisted getting to know his anger; he denied that it existed.

While mainstream psychology counsels people to recognize these forms of suppressed anger and offers strategies to deal with them, it often does this without encouraging an exploration of the underlying anger— the beast. As a result, it not only perpetuates but unwittingly increases suppression of the underlying anger and also ignores its message and power. This is what happened when Dr. Phil counseled Gretchen and her family. He exposed the family's denial of powerful feelings that had not been discussed, pointing out Gretchen's guilt, her sister's resentment, and the family's sustained silence. But then he immediately proceeded to help them "move past" these feelings, counseling that anger should be acknowledged and then let go. He prescribed meditation, prayer, and forgiveness to free them from their "attachment" to their anger.

However, the message and power of the individuals' underlying anger was never revealed or addressed. We did not know whether its source was pain that had never been fully appreciated, remorse that had never been expressed, rage that had never been understood, or relationship conflicts that had never been resolved. Nor did we know how the message and power of the family members' anger might have helped them change for the better. In short, we never got to meet the beast of anger or learn to appreciate its message and power.

For example, although Dr. Phil spoke openly with Gretchen about her guilt, something the family had never acknowledged, rather than exploring the underlying anger he coached her about accepting responsibility for her role in the car accident without continuing to blame herself and let guilt guide her actions. This approach ignored the power of Gretchen's anger, which had kept her feeling responsible for her sister's injury for fifteen years and prevented her from living her own life. Telling her to simply stop being motivated by this anger is more likely to further suppress her underlying anger than to free her from its grip. It also assumes that there is no reason to explore the message and power of the underlying anger.

Similarly, Dr. Phil saw that Gretchen's sister was suppressing her anger toward Gretchen and challenged her to acknowledge it, but rather than helping her explore these feelings he counseled her to move past them, practicing forgiveness as a way to "heal." This approach ignored the fact that the family's maintenance of silence made it unlikely that Gretchen's sister could ever acknowledge her feelings about having been in a traumatic accident. And it also did not acknowledge the power and potential in her anger, which individuals like Gretchen's sister may be able to use to turn their lives around. In addition, like many mainstream approaches that purport to eliminate anger without exploration of its message and power, it ignored what physicists call the law of conservation of energy, which states that energy can neither be created nor destroyed, only transformed.

Further, while Dr. Phil recognized the mother's tendency to try to control the family's pain for the sake of family harmony, he never explored her anger. Instead, he essentially aligned himself with her agenda, getting the sisters to move past their feelings without understanding or expressing them. By doing this, his counsel was more likely to encourage the mother to continue her controlling behavior rather than help her resolve the anger by encouraging the sisters to express their feelings about the mother's attempts to be controlling. When Gretchen's mother said that their father had forgiven Gretchen and Dr. Phil noted that the father had never actually said this, stressing that the mother was trying to control the sisters' feelings, it would have been a good moment for Dr. Phil to ask the sisters about their reaction to their mother's behavior, thereby opening the door to expressing their anger toward it. This kind of interaction would have made the mother more aware of how she keeps the family from addressing their feelings and made the sisters more aware of their own predisposition to suppressing anger rather than expressing their feelings.

Many mainstream approaches to anger inadvertently sanction the suppressive strategies utilized by such false peacemakers as Gretchen's mother, encouraging people to let go of their anger without exploring its message and power and thus keeping people who are potentially affected unaware of the important information and potential their anger conveys. Like Dr. Phil, such approaches fail to see the potential this advice has for creating circumstances where anger manifests in the destructive ways it did in Gretchen's family. In this way, mainstream psychology functions as Gretchen's mother did instead of showing people how to navigate through anger's fire, transforming it into life-giving energy without getting too burned. In effect, mainstream psychology throws the baby (the message and power of anger) out with the bathwater (the potential destructiveness of anger). It doesn't recognize that the powerful energy of anger does not simply disappear but rather has great potential for helping people transform their lives—an outcome that requires befriending the beast of anger.

DISCOVERING THE MESSAGE AND POWER OF ANGER

Befriending the beast of anger to discover its message and power requires a mind open to exploration and not prone to prejudgment. At the start, it is important to remember that encountering a trapped or caged beast gives us a different experience from meeting one that is free. A constrained animal might look ill, depressed, or potentially violent, while a free one is more likely to look intelligent and powerful, although it could be dangerous, in part because we don't know it well enough to interact with it properly. The same is true for the beast of anger. Investigating anger when it is suppressed can result in violence and destruction, and, when it is free, in an opportunity to discover its message and power.

Anger's message is revealed in an angry person's words, and its power is expressed in the angry person's behavior. Its message provides information critical to healing, while its power indicates energy the person can redirect to make the changes necessary to ultimately live a fulfilling life. Thus anger is not just an adversary but a worthy one with a message that can teach us and a power we can use for personal transformation.

One way anger provides a message and power for personal transformation is by unblocking access to feelings so the person gains increased freedom for catharsis. For example, like many people who have to cope with trauma, especially in families that promote silence and suppression, Gretchen's disabled sister avoided expressing her feelings. When this happens for long periods, a scab forms over the underlying wound, blocking access to these feelings. It can sometimes take the power of anger to break through this scab, allowing the underlying feelings to be expressed. Expressing angry emotions without trying to resolve them or subdue them can be very cathartic.

This method was particularly helpful to a woman I met at a workshop on the psychology of life-altering illness. She had lived with debilitating back pain for many years and seemed hostile toward people interested in her condition. Believing that her hostility was important, participants in the workshop encouraged her to express it. She said, "Do you know what it's like to live like this? To wake up every day and face physical pain, knowing I can't do the things I love, like going biking with my friends, and knowing I never will?" One workshop participant encouraged her further, saying, "No, tell us." Listening, we were deeply moved by her suffering. Not only did we not know what she had gone through but she herself was unaware of how much suffering she had habitually endured. She couldn't feel for herself until someone else felt for her first. Before her catharsis, she had communicated in a cold, stoic manner, and most of us responded accordingly, remaining distant and unfriendly. However, a her catharsis our hearts were open to her, and a palpable courage emanate from her. The message of her anger was her pain and suffering; the power of her anger broke through the lid of her suppression, allowing her to feel and express her pain and the rest of us to empathize with her. A similar healing power appeared to be latent in Gretchen's sister's anger.

Guilt, an expression of internalized anger, also sends an important message about people's needs, hopes, and dreams, and provides power for personal transformation that can be missed if we simply try to get them to stop feeling guilty. People tend to feel most guilty about doing things they actually *want* to do. For example, a woman may feel guilty about talking too much when, at a deeper level, she is tired of listening and not being heard. Or a man may feel guilty about getting sick and taking a day off from work when he has delayed his need for a break too long. Or a mother may feel guilty for not being there for her children all the time when, wishing she had help from her partner, she hasn't been able to ask for it. While it would be much more direct to get this information by simply asking a person what they need or want, people are rarely able to answer honestly.

Usually, the voice of guilt reveals specific important information about people's motivations and desires. For instance in the case of Gretchen, who punishes herself by not allowing herself to do things she loves, the voice of her guilt might be saying, "I won't let you do the things you love, like act or sing." We could then obtain further information by asking, "What else won't you let Gretchen do or say?" In this fashion, we would discover what would make Gretchen feel vital and joyful, information that is pure gold for anyone interested in living a fulfilling life.

Sometimes the message of anger, or its manifestation of guilt, can reveal an entirely new life direction, such as a career of service to atone for past harmful actions. For instance, when a client of mine who, as a gang member in his teens, had seriously hurt several people could not let go of his guilt, I asked, as if I were him addressing his guilt, "Dear guilt, what would you have me do to get off the hook?" The client replied angrily, "Become a teacher or writer and work with teens," discovering, because of this interaction, a new direction in his life. Similarly Gretchen, if she were to explore her guilt, might hear a message telling her she could atone by devoting her life to a cause that is meaningful to her. Unexplored, her guilt may remain until she is on a new life path since guilt usually persists until a person becomes free enough to make a meaningful change.

Harnessing anger's power for personal transformation can be profoundly healing. One way to support this outcome is by making people aware of how they are using the power of anger against themselves. For example, we might say to Gretchen, "You deserve to suffer for making your sister paralyzed for fifteen years. You are going to pay by losing your own life's passions and joy." Upon hearing how they subconsciously treat themselves, people see how destructive their guilt is and can begin taking back the power it exercises over their lives. If, on the other hand, we simply tell them to stop feeling guilty, they may experience less guilt but will not have harnessed the power to change their lives. Hearing anger's message and harnessing anger's power can also help transform relationships. Some people have a message for others that can only be revealed through their anger. For instance, healing Gretchen's relationship with her sister might be facilitated by supporting her sister's expression of anger toward her better than by counseling her sister to let go of her anger. In this case, the following scenario would likely occur: having observed Gretchen listening to her anger, demonstrating that she "gets it," and being moved as a result, Gretchen's sister would forgive her. In turn, if Gretchen were given an opportunity to speak out in her own defense, after years of having tried and convicted herself, and were supported in expressing her own feelings about the incident directly to her sister, she would have a much easier time letting go of her guilt.

Supporting Gretchen and her sister to express their underlying anger to each other would be more healing than another fifteen years of guilt, silence, and resentment. Their words would convey important messages about their deeper feelings, and the power of their anger might be the only force capable of breaking through the wall of silence they have created.

Mainstream psychology, which tends to focus on individuals, often ignores the possibility that anger's message can bring healing to relationships. In fact, while Dr. Phil suggests that Gretchen and her sister deal with her feelings individually through meditation, letting go, practicing forgiveness, or going to therapy, none of these strategies focuses directly on the anger's message and power. On the contrary, these strategies can promote avoiding difficult relationships instead of healing them.

Finally, anger's message and power can have great value for families. Anger in families, especially if it has been unexpressed for years or even generations, perpetuates undesirable dynamics that can send shock waves adversely affecting many individuals. In my experience of hearing people recount a painful dynamic of past generations, about half the time it resembles the current generation's dynamic. In fact, the current generation often appears to be charged with resolving the past generation's lingering traumas and preventing the same dynamic from recurring in future generations.

If we could investigate Gretchen's family's history, we might very well find a pattern of violence, accidents, tragedies, anger, and guilt preceding the current generation. An opportunity occurred to make the family aware of their pattern of suppressing anger when Gretchen's mother said their father had forgiven Gretchen even though he had never actually said this. Encouraging the sisters to share their reaction to their mother's behavior could have opened the door to expressing their anger about her controlling behavior. This kind of interaction would have not only made the mother more aware of how she keeps the family from addressing their feelings but also have made the sisters more aware of their own predisposition to suppress anger. Such awareness can be pivotal in shifting historical family patterns and paving the way for healing and transformation in the current and next generations.

CONCLUSION

Emily Dickinson wrote, "Anger as soon as fed is dead; 'Tis starving makes it fat."[2] In our culture, however, mainstream psychology regularly responds to anger in ways that starve it by suppressing it, thereby habitually treating anger as an enemy with nothing of value to offer. Unfortunately, this perspective too easily leads to superficial resolutions followed by an even more pronounced suppression of anger rather than to any exploration of anger's message and power.

Psychology can and must do better. Our understanding and interventions can be informed by the fact that the beast of anger comes riding in with a message on its back and a power in its stride, both of which can aid healing and transformation. The message and power of anger can be the driving forces of change, opening the door to new ways of resolving old conflicts, new ways of dealing with relationships, and new ways of living. The beast of anger, like an animal in the wild, can be met in a way that is both safe for people and respectful of the animal's nature. Creating such an encounter requires not only courage but an appreciation of anger's capacity to lead to greater happiness and fulfillment.

PART II

RELATIONSHIPS

Having It Out

Sustainable Alternatives to Compromise

Creating freedom, community,
and viable relationships has its costs.
It costs time and courage
to learn to sit in the fire of diversity.
—Arnold Mindell

M AINSTREAM PSYCHOLOGY, often naive about relationship conflict, focuses on finding resolutions and ignores underlying processes that are of potential long-term benefit to relationships. First, practitioners believe that conflict is defined by the content of people's disagreements. For example, if a couple says their differences are about money mainstream psychology generates a solution in financial terms; if their differences are about time spent at home, the proposed solution comes in the form of hours, days, and schedules. Second, practitioners believe that compromise is the key to resolving relationship conflict and essential to building sustainable relationships. This leads practitioners to act like arbiters, suggesting how people should compromise to resolve the conflict. People who don't follow these suggestions are treated as resistant or unreasonable. According to practitioners of mainstream psychology, it is not the solution or the approach that is inadequate when people don't arrive at or stick to a resolution but rather the people themselves.

Creating resolutions to relationship conflict by focusing on the content of disagreements and urging the people to compromise may result in a temporary victory but can limit people's perspective, making them small-minded and occupying them with issues like blame and ways of eliminating tension as soon as possible. As the poet Rilke says, "When we win it's with small things, and the triumph itself makes us small."[1]

The process-oriented psychology of Drs. Arnold and Amy Mindell offers an alternative to this paradigm. Instead of focusing on how to resolve conflict, as if it were a problem, it views conflict as something to embrace for purposes of growing and developing relationships. First, according to process-oriented psychology conflict is defined not by the content of people's disagreements but by the underlying processes, or relationship dynamics, which hold the potential for more meaningful and sustainable resolutions. For example, while a couple may have a conflict regarding money, the underlying process may have more to do with issues of power, life priorities, or ignored needs, and working with these issues may assist the couple in establishing new norms for relating that would help them in many additional situations.

Second, from the perspective of process-oriented psychology people's tendency to make compromises that are not right for them results in solutions that do not remain viable, whereas their unwillingness to compromise often provides information about their deeper concerns that can help in finding more lasting solutions. In fact, while mainstream psychology considers compromise a "win-win" situation, allowing both people to achieve some of what they want, many compromises, especially those involving deeper needs and values, are actually a "lose-lose" situation, causing both people to give up something they want, potentially resulting in a short-lived resolution. Finally, while mainstream psychology tries to restore harmony and the status quo when conflicts arise, process-oriented psychology focuses on how conflicts force people outside their comfort zones to make changes necessary for improving relationships in the future.

To better understand these different approaches, consider the following scenario. A man and a woman have a conflict about who should wash the dishes after a big Sunday night dinner. He says, somewhat annoyed and defensively, "I expect you to do it; you usually do. What's so different this time?" Feeling victimized by an unfair arrangement, she replies, "That's just the point. I always do the dishes. Why don't you do them for a change?"

A mainstream psychology approach, focusing on the content of the conflict—who should wash the dishes—would provide superficial resolutions based on sharing the chore. For example, some resolutions to the conflict might be to wash the dishes together that night or agree to share the task of dish washing in the future, alternating nights. A mainstream approach might even go one step further, encouraging this couple to empathize with each other's position to facilitate compromise and restore harmony. In this way, the man might find out that the woman feels taken for granted when it comes to doing the dishes, while the woman might discover that he feels taken for granted about other things that he routinely does, like taking out the garbage or mowing the lawn. They might come away understanding and appreciating each other more. Even so, resolving only the content of the "dishes conflict" minimizes the fact that it actually serves to highlight the couple's problems with communication.

From the perspective of process-oriented psychology, the process of the conflict—the way the couple works through issues based on assumptions and beliefs they have about themselves and each other—would reveal underlying relationship dynamics. In this case, working with the process of the conflict could lead to learning to communicate differently. For instance, prior to the conflict the woman did the dishes whether she wanted to or not and the man expected her to do the dishes without any discussion or negotiation. But by forcefully and directly suggesting changes in who does this chore she shifts the focus to relating differently to the man. As a result, he might respond to her protest by communicating more openly, or revealing more about his own needs and feelings instead of relying on unstated agreements to address his needs. In fact, if he does not he will likely become resentful, and the issue will arise again. Such development cannot take place if the focus is merely on the content of conflict, for it would maintain the couple's status quo, making it likely the same or a similar conflict would occur again later.

Although the underlying process of a conflict is often ignored because tackling it can be disturbing and destabilizing, focusing on it brings significant benefits that can nourish the seeds of more fundamental development. First, only when the underlying process is addressed are resolutions sustainable. Otherwise, conflicts reemerge in the same form with the same content or the same form with different content. It is like removing a tumor without also removing underlying cancer cells, making it likely the cancer will appear in other places and cause a host of other symptoms. Second, focusing on the underlying process supports a change in people and relationships that may address a range of issues to help in avoiding future conflicts. Thus this approach does more than resolve conflicts; it revitalizes relationships by creating greater intimacy, energy, and well-being.

THE *DR. PHIL* SHOW

An episode of the *Dr. Phil* show illustrated mainstream psychology's approach to resolving relationship conflict.[2] The guests on the show were a young couple about to be married who had come to Dr. Phil for help. The woman claimed she trusted her fiancé "completely," but a small bump on the way to the wedding betrayed other feelings. He wanted to have a bachelor party at a strip club, which she vehemently opposed. Dr. Phil saw willingness to compromise as key to resolving the conflict and, accordingly, tried to get the couple to compromise. "Marriage is a negotiation," Dr. Phil told them, explaining his belief that if a couple can't negotiate resolutions to conflicts that arise early in their relationship then it will be very difficult for them to negotiate future conflicts. He suggested that a compromise would include the man showing more sensitivity to the woman, perhaps holding the party at a club that does not have strippers, and the woman showing more trust toward the man, perhaps by understanding that her distrust of him is partly her own issue and therefore being more open to his bachelor party plans.

Although Dr. Phil's suggestions for compromise seem reasonable, the couple resisted following his advice. The woman insisted that the strip club was unacceptable, and the man seemed equally hesitant to change his plans even though now they were resisting not only a compromise with each other but Dr. Phil's efforts to persuade them. Nonetheless, instead of viewing their resistance as a meaningful underlying process, Dr. Phil treated it as a problem to overcome. Consequently, he dismissed the importance of their resistance and sent the couple off to negotiate further on their own while he worked with another couple. Later, when he checked in with them to see if they had progressed in finding a compromise, the man said, sarcastically, "Things are not going well for the men in the world"; and the woman, obviously frustrated, stated that they were still "debating." In fact, what appeared to Dr. Phil as resistance to compromise really indicated the presence of a powerful underlying process fueling the conflict, which remained unexplored. The perspective of mainstream psychology had led Dr. Phil to focus exclusively on the details of the bachelor party while ignoring the meaning of his guests' resistance to compromise, thus treating their resistance as a barrier to resolution rather than the doorway to a deeper and more sustainable resolution.

THE DANGERS OF COMPROMISING

While Dr. Phil and mainstream psychology perpetuate the idea that people must learn to compromise to build sustainable relationships, actually many people need to learn just the opposite—that compromising too readily builds unsustainable relationships. Compromising, especially when people are resistant to it, has two dangers. First, compromising too easily doesn't resolve conflict; it creates conflict. This is because when people compromise as a way of restoring harmony before expressing and defending their position they are not actually agreeing to a resolution, making it unlikely that any compromise will be sustainable. People in conflict need support not to be more compromising but rather to resist compromise until they have sufficiently expressed and defended their position. For example, when a group is trying to schedule a meeting, if they cannot find a time that works for everyone, one or more people may accommodate others by consenting to a time that is not best for them. Then frequently the conflict they avoided by being agreeable about the initial schedule surfaces again when their resistance reasserts itself, preventing them from arriving on time or from being present in mind and spirit, prompting others to accuse them of being unreliable or unfocused. Such people don't need to practice being more reliable or focused but instead less compromising so they make agreements they are willing and able to honor. In fact, it is those around them who need to be more responsible by noticing their resistance to the schedule and ensuring that a real resolution has been arrived at instead of an unsustainable compromise.

Second, many people make compromises at the beginning of a relationship, before any conflict takes place, thinking of them as sacrifices required to build a sustainable relationship. However, upon making such compromises without considering their own happiness and well-being they may later become resentful and give mixed messages about keeping their agreements, resulting in a conflict. Such an eventual conflict cannot be resolved by encouraging further compromise; it must be resolved by supporting the person to identify and defend their needs so they learn to connect their resistance to the underlying issues.

For instance, a man with whom I once worked complained of having regular relationship conflicts; he resisted and asserted himself, even as he told himself to let go, relax, and be more understanding. I asked him if there was something in the relationship to which he was agreeing without really meaning it, because he felt he had little or no choice. After some reflection, he said that he was agreeing to spend all of his time working—doing chores, performing at his job, and taking care of the family—with no time for fun. He was never asked to make this sacrifice but, like many people who begin a long-term relationship, had agreed to a set of unexamined expectations about what it takes to build a sustainable relationship with-out critically evaluating them in terms of his own needs. When he told his spouse about this, she said she also wanted to spend more time having fun. They both realized they had made compromises that were untenable and began having more fun together. The man had remained resistant to com-promise until using it to better assess his own needs, and his resistance had indeed been meaningful, providing essential information that improved his relationship.

In general, at the beginning of relationships people unconsciously make certain compromises they believe will sustain those relationships without assessing them in terms of their personal needs, priorities, and values. If these compromises have not been fully and consciously agreed to, resistance arises, although it often remains unexpressed until a later conflict provides an opportunity for the resistance to be addressed and the underlying needs, priorities, and values to be embraced. During the time people are resistant to compromises they need a psychological approach that goes beyond helping them make compromises to helping them explore the deeper underlying processes related to their disagreements. Assisting them in building a sustainable relationship will then call for discussion of the underlying needs, priorities, and values of both partners. Such couples invariably find that the presenting conflict is relatively unimportant, and they feel better understood, happier, more hopeful, and more open to compromise in the future.

This dynamic might be relevant to the couple on the *Dr. Phil* show. The fiancé's refusal to compromise with regard to his bachelor party plans might represent resistance to more fundamental sacrifices he is fearful of making once he gets married. Based on his comment, "Things are not going well for the men in the world," and his insistence on having the party at a strip club, he probably associates sacrificing his plan with sacrificing aspects of his masculinity. Perhaps he believes that his bachelor party is his last chance to express a fundamental aspect of his nature and that there will be no opportunity in his married life to be bawdy, loud and sexual, or whatever he associates with masculine behavior. If this is the case, instead of encouraging him to be compromising it might be more fruitful to ask him what sacrifices he believes he will have to make once he is married.

Then we might need to encourage him to consciously integrate the parts of himself he associates with masculine behavior into his relationship to avoid building into it reasons for his relationship to fail. Thus a more sustainable resolution to the "bachelor party problem" would likely have little or nothing to do with the details of it and more to do with a change in his assumptions about the sacrifices he needs to make in his marriage and the kind of relationship he wants with his future wife. While his resistance to compromise with regard to the bachelor party may seem petty, it could reveal important information about his needs and might very well save his marriage.

Similarly, while his fiancée resists compromising, she, too, may need to assess sacrifices that she believes she must make to build a sustainable relationship. Her penchant for setting limits and unwillingness to change her mind about aspects of the bachelor party indicates she may have un-identified fundamental needs, priorities, or values that must not be sacri-ficed. Until she identifies and asserts those aspects of herself, the bachelor party arrangements may seem to her like her last chance to do so. More likely, it is her deeper underlying needs, priorities, and values that require negotiation than details about the bachelor party.

While people's resistance to compromise in relationships can reveal important information about their fundamental needs, priorities, and values, the unique manner of their resistance generally determines how best to support it. For example, the fiancée on the *Dr. Phil* show resisted compromise by setting limits and refusing to negotiate. Supporting her resistance could best be accomplished by encouraging her to go further in this direction. For instance, we could ask her to feel the power and con-viction expressed in her immovability, identify assumptions that might prevent her from expressing her power, and help her see her power in a more positive light. In this way, her resistant style, which mainstream psychology and Dr. Phil consider a barrier to resolution, would actually become an ally empowering her to avoid pursuing harmony before she has spoken up and not make sacrifices to which she cannot honestly agree. Thus both her resistance to compromise and the way she resists could be seen as meaningful.

The fiancé has his own way of resisting compromise. He insists on what he wants and stands up for what he believes are men's desires and styles. However, as insistent as he is on aspects of the bachelor party he would likely be very shy about asserting his needs "as a man" directly to his fiancée regarding other situations. We could support his resistance by asking him to feel the nature of his desire and tenacity, identify assumptions about what he thinks might prevent him from expressing himself this way, and affirm the value of this aspect of his nature. Thus resistance to compromise can be seen not as a barrier to overcome but as an ally, helping people assert their needs and desires in ways that will further their efforts in building sustainable relationships.

CONCLUSION

Mainstream psychology sees the content of relationship conflicts and learning to compromise as keys to resolving disagreements, making practitioners behave more like mediators or arbiters than psychologists. However, focusing on the underlying processes reveals crucial information about needs, priorities, and values that can be of greater benefit to relationships over time. Mainstream psychology works to deescalate conflict often before people state their needs, defend their positions, or even discover what their conflict is actually about. It tries to get people to chill out or, as Dr. Phil says, let "cooler heads prevail." However, while this might prove to be a short-term fix it frequently makes people miss long-term benefits.

When we instead focus on a conflict's underlying process, we see that resolutions, especially to conflicts where long-term relationships are at stake, are only partly about agreeing on terms and conditions. To be sustainable, resolutions need to also be about people coming to know themselves and each other more fully, recognizing that when people resist compromise they have good reasons for doing so and that uncovering these reasons yields valuable information that can improve relationships. Thus relationship conflicts are not merely problems to resolve; like arrows, they point to the next step on the paths of relationships. In trying to resolve relationship conflicts, people are not only looking for resolutions that restore harmony and the status quo; they are actually seeking to come to know themselves and improve the fundamental aspects of their relationships.

Conflict gives rise to the desire for truth, integrity, dignity, love, and intimacy. Psychology should serve these profound human longings by teaching people to see conflict as a great crucible for change and development.

Relationship Conflict

What's Gender Got to Do with It?

> [W]hen a man was considering divorce, his common statement was,
> "No matter what I do it is not enough to make her happy." Rarely did I hear
> women say this. Instead women would often complain: He doesn't listen;
> he is inattentive, he is no longer romantic . . .
>
> —John Gray

IN MAINSTREAM CULTURE, there are many assumptions about how men and women should behave in relationship with each other. These assumptions lead to patterns of behavior and create standards that encourage or discourage the expression of particular feelings. I call these patterns and standards "traditional gender roles." Mainstream psychology tends to reinforce these assumptions, standards, and roles. Perhaps no one has articulated assumptions about traditional gender roles better than John Gray, author of one of the most popular books ever written, *Men Are from Mars, Women Are from Venus*. According to Gray, men are thinkers and women are feelers; men strive to solve problems, and women complain so they will be listened to; men deal with stress by being alone, and women deal with stress by talking; and men are happy when they accomplish goals, and women are happy when they feel nurtured.[1] Mainstream psychology views these differences between men and women as predictable and invariable, assuming that if we want to avoid conflict and have happy relationships we must understand and conform to them.

However, these assumptions about gender roles are as much a function of cultural stereotypes and biases as men's and women's natural inclinations. In addition, while mainstream psychology believes these differences are static, actually they are in flux and have undergone profound change over the years. Even the most traditional assumption, that men are providers and women are more dependent, is hardly applicable today. Thus, while it is clear that large numbers of people find this perspective compelling, as time goes on it is becoming less true, pressuring increasingly more people to conform to a way of relating that causes difficulty and distress instead of ease and wellness. Assumptions about gender roles not only create constraining norms of behavior but are responsible for relationship difficulties. Rather than help us understand each other, these traditional patterns often cause misunderstanding and blind us to our own and our partner's diverse qualities. Furthermore, instead of providing a template that resolves tension, assumptions about gender roles create one-size-fits-all norms that result in various symptoms of dis-ease, from depression and stress to isolation and conflict, as people try to play roles that distort their true nature and prevent the natural flowering of their relationships. We need to be aware of our assumptions about gender roles so that in our relationships we minimize conflict and maximize manifestations of our love for others.

THE *DR. PHIL* SHOW

One episode of the *Dr. Phil* show that focused on a married couple whose relationship was based on traditional assumptions about gender roles illustrated how such assumptions can create conflict.[2] This African American man and woman had enjoyed a sweet romance on the way to the altar. "He had swept me off my feet," the wife told Dr. Phil, but she complained that the romance was now gone and argued that her husband was to blame for the drought—no more flowers or dinners out. She wanted

him to woo her again the way he had at the beginning of their relationship, starting with taking her out to dinner more often. However, while
the husband didn't disagree with her about the lack of romance in their
relationship, he protested the effort required to provide romance in addition to dealing with the mounting stresses and responsibilities he faced,
including a new baby, car, house, and business. Nonetheless, he said he
would do his best to fulfill his obligations, asking only that she give him a
list of restaurants from which to choose. But from her point of view it was
also his job to make any arrangements regarding romantic evenings so she
refused to provide the list.

This couple had structured their relationship according to traditional
gender roles. The husband was the romancer; the wife was the romanced.
He was the actor; she was the passive recipient. And while they both had
worked at the beginning of the relationship, soon after having a child
the wife had become a full-time stay-at-home mother, while the husband
had become the sole provider. He was also goal oriented and dealt with
his stress alone. She complained in order to be listened to and looked
for nurturance and romance to make her happy. In the language of best-
selling author John Gray, he was indeed from Mars, and she was from
Venus. Now that a conflict had arisen, they viewed it through the lens
these roles provided. While the husband felt overextended, he believed it
was his duty to do whatever it took to satisfy his wife, never considering it
her task. And although the wife spoke freely about her dissatisfactions she
didn't see that she could do anything about her needs other than complain,
for instance, that she could initiate romance by taking her husband out to
dinner or provide him with support regarding his stress.

Consistent with mainstream psychology, Dr. Phil focused on the content of the conflict between the husband and wife instead of exploring
the underlying process of the conflict. Accordingly, he viewed the lack of

romance as the problem and attempted to get the couple to compromise—
the husband to work harder at romancing his wife and the wife to provide
the list of restaurants. However, while on the surface the conflict appeared
to be about the lack of romance, at a deeper level the conflict was about
how the couple's rigid traditional gender roles dictated what the husband
and wife could ask from each other and how direct they could be in
communicating their needs. Thus the husband could neither directly ask
for the wife's emotional support nor say that her request was too much for
him; and she could not make dinner plans. In ignoring that the couple's
insistence on playing traditional gender roles was a cause of the conflict,
Dr. Phil could not recommend that freeing themselves from these roles
could help resolve the conflict.

Instead, Dr. Phil suggested ways the couple could resolve the conflict
in conformity to these roles, even though his guests gave him ample reason
to believe the roles were no longer suitable for them. He saw the husband
as having two jobs: his work outside the home and his work inside the
home. But he suggested that the husband had no right to complain, citing research indicating that being a homemaker and taking care of a child
is like having two jobs. Rather than treating the husband's complaint as
resistance to his role, he delegitimized his feelings of being overburdened
and declared that it was the husband's failings, not the inadequacies of
cultural biases, that had caused the conflict. He graded the husband on his
two jobs, giving him high marks on meeting his financial responsibilities
and "Ds or Fs" on providing romance, support, and attention to his wife.
He told the husband that it was his job to make his wife happy and that
she should have higher self-esteem every time they interacted.

Similarly, Dr. Phil persuaded the wife to conform to her gender role.
While he challenged her mindset by telling her "this is a partnership" and
by asking her to make the minimal compromise of providing her husband

with a list of restaurants, he never also said that the wife had a reciprocal responsibility to make her husband happy, that the husband had a need for support and romance, or that her relationship was like a job to be graded.

Instead, he sent a clear message that the wife had every right to expect more romance and it was her husband's job to meet her needs, communicating to women that they deserve to be romanced but also that women are to be passive recipients, affirming the wife's gender-defined expectations and lack of power to meet her own needs. In short, Dr. Phil acted as an enforcer of the mainstream assumptions regarding gender roles in relationships.

Not only did Dr. Phil encourage the husband and wife to conform to traditional gender roles by defining their responsibilities and legitimizing the needs that correspond to those roles, but also his assumptions and beliefs affected the way he communicated to them. From the beginning, he took on the role of advocate for the wife, treating her as if she and not her husband needed his understanding and support. First, he did this by defining the conflict, and thereby any resolution, in terms of the wife's complaint about the lack of romance. While the husband had an equally compelling complaint about the burden of being a sole provider in a marriage involving a new baby, house, and business, Dr. Phil treated his complaint as if it were an illegitimate justification for not meeting his wife needs. He turned a deaf ear to how the husband kept talking about "trying hard" and "doing the heavy lifting," phrases that many men use to indicate the extent of their suffering and their need for support. Even when the husband directly asked for Dr. Phil's understanding and suggestions about how to manage the pressure of maintaining his work and relationship Dr. Phil gave no such advice, focusing instead on the wife's complaint as if it were the only problem that needed to be resolved.

And even though the wife, compared to the husband, was more assertive, articulate, and immovable in declaring her needs and dissatisfactions, Dr. Phil treated her as if she needed his help to communicate her position. He advocated for her rather than facilitating the relationship, treating the wife as the weaker party needing his support instead of viewing the husband and wife as equals. In this way, his assumptions and beliefs, expressed through his style and behavior, promoted traditional gender roles as opposed to helping this couple free themselves from them. In effect, Dr. Phil acted like a knight riding in to save the damsel in distress, all the while patronizing the wife and dismissing the husband's real concerns.

A PROCESS-ORIENTED ALTERNATIVE PERSPECTIVE ON RELATIONSHIP CONFLICT

Process-oriented psychology provides an alternative perspective to Dr. Phil's mainstream viewpoint that the husband and wife's conflict should be resolved by conforming to their assigned gender roles. This perspective, which focuses on the process underlying the conflict as the path to resolution, would take change in the husband's behavior as indicative of an underlying urge for transformation that needed to be supported. For example, his behavior indicated that while he is still fulfilling the role of financial provider he is moving away from fulfilling the role of romancer. "His idea of romance is paying the bills," the wife asserted. "It's hard to be romantic when you have to work all the time," he responded. In essence, the husband was beginning to resist playing the role of romancer and showing symptoms of distress as a result of trying to conform to his traditional gender role, complaining not only about his unbearable workload but about the constraints of his traditional gender role. From this perspective, the cause of the conflict would not be the husband's inadequacy in conforming to his assigned gender role but the inadequacy of the role itself.

This perspective also would take changes in his communication style, especially the tone and feeling expressed, as indicative of his urge for transformation. For example, the fact that his voice sounded exhausted and he spoke repeatedly about how hard he was trying, pleading with his wife and Dr. Phil to understand was more expressive of vulnerability and need for support than of a person who needed to "buck up" and do his job.

Viewing the situation from this perspective would radically change the nature of the interventions required to resolve the conflict. Instead of confronting the husband's failure to perform and challenging him to try harder, we would encourage him to talk more about his feelings of being overburdened, trusting that they were meaningful and not justifications. We would help him identify the weakness in his voice as an expression of his need for support. We would explore how he might let go of some of his responsibilities, and we would challenge the traditional beliefs that might make it hard for him to do so. In short, we would help him become freer to act in ways traditionally considered to be aspects of the female role.

We would also consider the wife's behavior and communication style from this alternative perspective. We would view change in the wife's behavior as indicative of an underlying urge for transformation that needed to be supported. For example, although she once was the passive recipient of her husband's efforts to romance her, she was now asking for what she wanted and becoming less accommodating, refusing to fulfill Dr. Phil's and her husband's request for a list of restaurants. We would also take changes in her communication style, especially the tone and feeling expressed, as indicative of her urge for transformation. Her communication style had become more assertive and demanding, expressing more power and authority, showing that she was beginning to behave outside her traditional gender role.

Working to resolve the conflict, we would challenge her to do more than provide restaurant options by encouraging her to organize romantic dinners herself or, better yet, step into the role of romancer. In addition, we would help her identify with the power in her voice, encouraging the expression of her authority in all areas of their relationship and challenging her traditional beliefs that might deem such expression inappropriate. In short, we would help her become freer to act in ways traditionally considered aspects of the male role. Helping them both become freer with regard to these gender roles would allow them to not only resolve the romance problem but revitalize their relationship.

Thus process-oriented psychology would see the wife's complaints about lack of romance, the husband's resistance to playing his role, as well as the conflict itself as indicating the couple's urge to develop their relationship into one that is more fluid and equal. Rather than regarding the lack of romance, the husband's needs and feelings, and the wife's unwillingness to compromise as problems to be overcome, it would consider these positive signs of growth. Instead of encouraging them to conform to traditional gender roles, it would view their freedom from them as the resolution.

CONCLUSION

While many people begin their relationships in accordance with traditional gender roles, being confined to these roles prohibits people from expressing behaviors and feelings outside of them, often causing conflict and unhappiness. Frequently, it takes illness, accidents, depression, affairs, or alcohol or other substance abuse to "help" men and women depart from these traditional gender roles when they are unable to resist more consciously. The fact that Viagra is the best-selling drug ever suggests that men don't easily take a break from their assumed responsibilities. And the fact that women are culturally chastised for expressing their power and authority suggests that there are still potent forces opposing women's freedom and sovereignty. Both women and men have a common enemy—a system promoting limited roles, opportunities, and styles of interaction—and mainstream psychology works within this system, invariably colluding with it.

The dilemma of being constrained and inhibited by rigid gender roles is not limited to heterosexual couples but can also occur with same-sex couples who divide the two roles between partners. In this case, when the gender roles are static and rigid the same conflicts emerge. The partner who takes on the male role—the doer and problem solver—experiences a sense of self-worth and pride at the beginning of a relationship but may develop resentment as time goes on. The partner who takes on the female role—the feeler, the receptive one, the one needing nurturance—often feels valued and taken care of at the beginning of a relationship but may later show signs of disempowerment and an inclination to express more power.

In contrast to mainstream psychology's practice of pressuring people to maintain traditional gender roles, process-oriented psychology sees resistance to playing these roles as suggestive of the need for a new paradigm in relationships. This approach trusts that people's behaviors are meaningful and listens to the tone and feeling of their communications, turning attention away from the content of conflicts and toward the underlying processes of the conflicts. From this perspective, resistance to aspects of traditional gender roles provides important information about urges for freedom of action and expression.

Relationships are expressions of our most profound hopes for love and connection. With the proper support and nourishment, they blossom into expressions of authenticity, beauty, and purpose. Mainstream psychology, as expressed by John Gray, Dr. Phil, and others, provides a template for understanding relationship difficulties that models biases about gender roles and promotes a narrow range of these diverse forms of ex-pression. Consequently, people who look to its advocates for wisdom and direction are in danger of remaining blind to the ways in which traditional gender roles limit their freedom and feed the underlying causes of conflict. Instead, we need a psychology that promotes a broader range of gender behavior in relationships and encourages a better understanding of fun-damental relationship issues, leading to fewer conflicts and more fulfilling relationships in the future.

Rank Dynamics

The Anatomy of an Affair

Rankism is an assertion of superiority.
It's what "Somebodies" do to "nobodies."
Or, more precisely, it is what people who think they're
Somebodies do to people they take for nobodies.
—Robert Fuller

SOME PEOPLE HAVE MORE POWER THAN OTHERS. Arnold Mindell, Ph.D., says they have more "rank,"[1] a term that conjures up the hierarchy of authority in the military. Rank differences determine the extent to which a person can dominate, intimidate, or dictate in relationships or groups. There are various types of rank differences in our everyday lives, not all of which are as obvious as those in the military. For example, most of us would agree that greater size or physical strength gives an individual higher rank when it comes to feats of strength or physical intimidation, but few people realize that height creates rank not only physically but also psychologically and thus is one of the best predictors of success in the corporate workplace. As Timothy A. Judge and Daniel M. Cable, who researched and reviewed over forty studies of the relationship between height and workplace success, state, "The process of literally 'looking down on others' may cause one to be more confident."[2]

Further, it has been statistically confirmed that in terms of success in the marketplace gender creates rank differences, with women earning around 80 percent of what men earn for the same job, even when they have similar backgrounds, education, and skills. While most managers would assert that they are not gender biased, nonetheless in this study and others gender was the basis for differential treatment giving men more rank than women in the workplace.[3] Moreover, higher-rank people who perpetrate such injustice are protected by their own and the culture's blindness to this bias.

Beyond providing a sense of authority and ability, rank differences also have a powerful effect on the way people react to and communicate with one another. Rank differences create predictable communication patterns between people even if they are unaware of the dynamic and if the rank differences are subtle, such as between husband and wife, or people of different financial status or with different levels of self-esteem. Rank differences can make some people feel secure and free to speak, and others insecure, inhibited, out of control, or even depressed. I once coached a manager who had no understanding of the effects of rank differences in giving feedback to an employee he found particularly difficult. The manager had concluded that the employee was too insecure to accept his negative feedback since he saw no other reason for his employee's subsequent anxiety or fears. But when I asked the manager what it was like to get feedback from his boss he spoke about his difficulties sleeping the night before, his fear of being defensive, and his need for support afterward—the same behaviors he had criticized as psychological weaknesses, unaware that they resulted from rank differences.

Not surprisingly, people with higher rank are more likely to speak than listen, act confident rather than defensive, follow their intuition and impulses rather than worry about what other people think, tell jokes rather than laugh at them, and rely on their own authority rather than look to others for affirmation of their views and ideas. Such behavior can easily be seen in children, who are more likely to look to people of higher rank, such as parents or teachers, for approval; be fearful of their disapproval or criticism; and listen rather than give advice.

By contrast, people with lower rank are more likely to feel challenged, bullied, or abused by higher-rank individuals or to act out or be depressed; to turn their reactions to such mistreatment into competition with others of similar or lower rank than to stand up to the higher-rank people; and to retaliate against individuals with similar or lower rank, in safer, less direct ways and often unconsciously. For example, a man after being pushed around by his boss might come home from work and retaliate against his children, wife, or dog. Or children who have been abused might abuse animals, younger siblings, or their own children even years later.

Similarly, when members of a minority or disenfranchised subculture are abused by members of a majority group or the mainstream culture they are likely to retaliate against members of their own group instead of the group responsible. For example, research shows that when bullies are women they choose other women as their prey in 71 percent of cases, and 70 percent of women who are bullies in the workplace usually bully other women as opposed to men.[4] Rather than question why this occurs, men knowingly smile at each other, and women are all too eager to confirm this fact with stories that further support the unspoken assumptions: that women with power treat other women worse than men treat women and, by extension, that men's mistreatment of women isn't all that bad. Robert W. Fuller, in his enlightening book *Somebodies and Nobodies: Overcoming the Abuse of Rank,* called this abusive use of rank "rankism."[5]

Although such patterns of communication and retaliation are easily explained by rank differences, practitioners of mainstream psychology are often unaware of the impact of rank differences, leading them to over-look rank-related issues, such as viewing a lower-rank person's or group's behavior and feelings as pathological rather than focusing on underlying rank differences unrelated to their intrapsychic conditions. Pathologizing people with lower rank may lead such practitioners to focus on the roles people with equal or lower rank play in conflict and ignore the roles played by those with higher rank—for instance, focusing on the roles of employees, children, women, or blacks while ignoring the roles of bosses, parents, men, or whites. In addition, practitioners of mainstream psychology may fail to ask individuals of higher rank to be more conscious of and responsible for the way their rank impacts other people or fail to help people with lower rank claim their power. Finally, such practitioners can be blind to the power dynamics their own rank establishes with their clients, increasing the possibility of reenacting a past injury caused by rank differences.

THE *DR. PHIL* SHOW

An episode of the *Dr. Phil* show focusing on the relationship fallout resulting from an affair illustrated how power dynamics can significantly impact the behavior and communication of individuals.[6] Dr. Phil's guests were two women; one woman was married to a man who had had an affair with the other woman. The other woman was pregnant as a result of the affair with the husband, who had declined Dr. Phil's invitation to join them. While Dr. Phil made no mention of the rank differences between the parties, the statuses created by the profession, gender, and economic disparities between them were obvious. The husband was a doctor; the "other woman" was a nurse. In the medical profession, relationships between doctors and nurses often follow the communication patterns between higher-rank and lower-rank people, especially when the doctor is a man and the nurse is a woman. The husband and wife's relationship was also marked by rank differences. He was a highly paid, highly educated professional, while she was a stay-at-home mother—distinctions that have potent rank implications in our culture. In addition, the wife had been betrayed, an act that had victimized her, amplifying the rank differences that already existed between her and her husband.

On a prior show, Dr. Phil had met with the husband and wife. At that time, the husband had said that the affair was supposed to be a one-time event but he was still dating the "other woman." When Dr. Phil asked the wife about her husband's betrayal, she didn't show much anger toward him, instead saying that he had an addiction. However, when talking about the other woman the wife expressed considerable anger and outrage. The wife's justification of the behavior of her husband, a person of higher rank, and hostility toward the other woman, a person of equal or lower rank, is a pattern typically caused by rank dynamics.

On the show with the two women, Dr. Phil clearly believed that confronting the other woman would be healing for the wife. He initiated the confrontation by asking the other woman, "Don't you have any standards?" and "What gives you the right?" Siding with the wife against her, Dr. Phil and his audience created an atmosphere conducive more to retaliation than to open and honest discussion.

In addition, the husband's absence from the show set up the two women to retaliate against each other for their experiences of violation, competition, and betrayal, taking the spotlight off the husband. Dr. Phil's agenda, helping the wife confront the other woman, and his expression of moral outrage at the other woman, ensured that not only the women on stage but also his audience would avoid focusing on the role the husband played in their predicament. Thus, the two women were unlikely to discover how the husband similarly mistreated them; form a solidarity that would make future mistreatment of each other less likely; or become aware of how, due to lower-rank status, they had been pitted against each other instead of retaliating against the husband.

PITTING LOWER-RANK PEOPLE AND GROUPS AGAINST EACH OTHER

Most people in our culture, as well as many practitioners of mainstream psychology, commonly ignore rank differences and the way lower-rank individuals can be pitted against each other to the exclusion of any higher-rank individuals involved who should be held accountable for circumstances. For example, a couple I knew had three children: James, the oldest; Sam, about two years younger; and Jill, about two years younger than Sam. The father, who was a doctor, pushed his children hard in both scholastics and sports, making the children redo their homework until he found no errors and participate in sports to win. While Sam thrived as a result of their father's efforts, for James and Jill, who were more sensitive children, scholastics and sports were harder. One day, as the parents sat in the living room with friends and family members, the father called the children to him and began praising Sam for his excellent performance in school and sports but expressing no praise for the other two children, insinuating that they were lacking.

Subsequently, the children began competing, putting each other down, and being jealous of each other. Sam often spoke derisively about James. James thought Sam was obnoxious. Jill simply withdrew and later developed a bitter streak that many people found unlikable. None of the children challenged the way their father had pitted them against each other, put them down, and compared them openly in front of others, instead retaliating against those of equal or lower rank—each other. In addition, while most of the father's friends and family were critical of the way the children treated each other, and some could see that the father's critical demeanor had rubbed off on his children, few could see that they behaved consistent with being of lower rank and none held the father responsible for the children's behavior.

The same was true for the two women on the *Dr. Phil* show. Neither Dr. Phil nor, apparently, his audience noted the way rank dynamics had set these women up to compete with each other and retaliate against each other instead of against the husband.

THE "INVISIBILITY" OF HIGHER-RANK PEOPLE

According to rank dynamics, when a person from a disenfranchised group (a group with lower rank) is in a conflict with a person from a dominant group (a group with higher rank), it often turns into a conflict between members of the disenfranchised group. Like the husband on the *Dr. Phil* show, the group with the higher rank simply fades into the background, essentially becoming invisible, creating the ideal condition for them to feel superior and be judgmental, as well as avoid all accountability for the circumstances. Unless their invisibility is noted and discussed, all those around them will focus attention on the infighting among the disenfranchised group, remain blind to the role played by the higher-rank person or group in the conflict, and feel superior to and judge those involved in the conflict. (The way some people throw around the term "cat fight" when two women are engaged in conflict is a well-known example of this phenomenon.) In short, those charged with witnessing the conflict become functionally just like the higher-rank person.

This is exactly what happened on the *Dr. Phil* show. The fact that the husband did not appear and Dr. Phil didn't mention the husband's role in the conflict made it easy for Dr. Phil and the audience to forget that he even existed, and, empathizing with the betrayed wife, focus their own anger and judgment on the other woman. In a way, they behaved just like the husband, only this time the other woman, instead of the wife, was humiliated. Moreover, rank dynamics dictates that, as a result, the other woman will probably eventually retaliate against someone with equal or lower rank, increasing the likelihood that the betrayal, competition, and jealousy between women in general will be carried forward.

An example of this kind of rank dynamic arose in a group conflict resolution seminar. It started when a man and woman were engaged in a conflict. While she was about to respond to the man's words, another man interrupted her in an effort to "help" her explain her viewpoint. While he said he was trying to be supportive, she chided him for being sexist, saying that she felt his actions were patronizing. Almost instantly another woman spoke up challenging the first woman, saying that the man was indeed just trying to help. She expressed her appreciation for men like him and said that too many women were attacking men in the name of feminism. Soon other women sided with the first woman, agreeing that the man had been patronizing, while still others sided with the second woman, agreeing that women have become too critical of men. As a result, the man, as well as the other men in the group, who had higher rank in this situation, virtually faded into the background as if they had been given magic cloaks that rendered them invisible. Some of the men admired the women's strength, and others felt defended by the women who challenged the feminists. But all of them felt safer because the women in the conflict were focused on each other—and the collective blindness to rank dynamics had prevented anyone from questioning what had transpired.

RANK DYNAMICS AND EVALUATION

Rank not only sets up conflict between lower-rank people and groups and causes the "invisibility" of higher-rank people, it also determines whose evaluations count, dictating that the evaluations higher-rank people make of lower-rank people are of greater importance. Bosses evaluate employees, teachers evaluate students, and parents evaluate children. Certainly, people of lower rank evaluate those with higher rank, but their evaluations are usually less consequential. For example, when parents evaluate or criticize their children it has great significance, but when children evaluate or criticize their parents the significance is minimal. In addition, while the evaluations of higher-rank people are likely to be considered objective and worthy of response, the evaluations of lower-rank people are often attributed to their rebelliousness, jealousy, or impulsive feelings as opposed to their valid perceptions of the higher-rank individuals.

This aspect of rank dynamics was in evidence on the *Dr. Phil* show. The husband, on the earlier show, had compared his wife to the other woman sexually and found his wife inferior. The husband behaved in a way consistent with his higher rank, with the unconscious assumption that evaluating these women was an acceptable activity and based on somewhat objective criteria. The wife, consistent with her lower rank, was devastated when told that she was less of a lover than the other woman. The audience reacted with outrage in response to the wife's "grade" but not in response to the women being evaluated in the first place. Even though the husband's ethics, sensibilities, and care for others were clearly in question, Dr. Phil and the audience inadvertently confirmed his higher rank and right to evaluate the two women sexually. They simply disagreed with his evaluation of the wife as an inferior lover.

The insult of the husband evaluating the women at all was missed because of the unconscious assumption that evaluation of lower-rank people by higher-rank people is a reasonable, objective activity. Rather than challenging this dynamic and pointing out the insult to both women, and women in general, Dr. Phil continued the evaluation process. He took out a picture of the other woman and showed it to the wife in an effort to prove that the wife was indeed more attractive. Also, he didn't see how he condoned and perpetuated the hurtful competition between the women as well as the legacy of superiority held by those of higher rank.

Even if we are accepting of Dr. Phil's more benevolent motives, the show still inadvertently reenacted the activity of a higher-rank person evaluating lower-rank people.

Despite these unbeneficial and inequitable aspects of rank dynamics, we can learn to effectively deal with them in several ways: by maintaining awareness of these dynamics, which is more difficult to do from a higher-rank position, because of feeling more at ease, than from a lower-rank position, because of feeling intimidated, insecure, or defensive; by having empathy for those in lower-rank positions and trying to understand how they are affected by the actions of those in higher-rank positions; and by questioning people with higher rank, thereby not letting them become invisible and unaccountable.

CONCLUSION

People in our culture, like Dr. Phil's audience, readily empathize with those who have experienced the pain of a spouse or partner's infidelity. However, the wounds caused by unconscious rank dynamics are often less obvious and require greater awareness to be revealed. Rank dynamics often pit victims against each other, turn the focus away from perpetrators of injurious behavior, and promote evaluation of people with lower rank by people with higher rank. In addition, as we saw on the *Dr. Phil* show, rank dynamics can even be unconsciously reenacted and encouraged in others by those whose intention is to heal not harm.

PART III

DIETS AND BODY IMAGE

Married to Dieting

Banking on Failure

Look, you've got to love yourself not only in the abstract;
you've got to love your big lips; you've got to love your flat nose;
you've got to love your skin, hands all the way down.

—Toni Morrison

AMERICANS ARE BOMBARDED WITH MESSAGES that they need to lose weight, but the truth is that many of us, especially women, need to either stop dieting or reassess our motivations for dieting. Messages that beauty and self-worth can be measured by body size result in the following alarming facts: while about 25 percent of women are overweight, 75 percent say they are overweight and feel ashamed of their "failure" to change.[1] Young girls between ages eleven and seventeen are more afraid of becoming fat than they are of nuclear war, cancer, or losing their parents.[2] Ninety percent of high school girls diet regularly, even though less than 20 percent are over the weight recommended by standard height-weight charts.[3] Negative body image is associated with suicide for girls but not for boys.[4] Fifty percent of girls between ages nine and ten feel better about themselves if they are dieting.[5] The most common behavior that leads to an eating disorder is dieting.[6] Thirty-five percent of "normal dieters" progress to pathological dieting.[7] About 8 million Americans have eating disorders, 7 million of them women.[8] Almost 40 percent of women who smoke say they do so to lose weight.[9] Seventy-five percent of women choose an ideal body size that is 10 to 20 percent underweight.[10] And women's magazines have ten times more articles and ads promoting weight loss than men's magazines.[11]

Clearly many individuals, especially women, have internalized a powerful and critical self-consciousness about their bodies and weight. Negative body image, which often drives us to diet, is a form of shame fostered by families; ever-present media images; ignorant cultural assumptions about women, beauty, and health; denial of the prevalence and role of sexual abuse in creating body shame; and a burgeoning $60 billion dieting industry ready to exploit all believers, banking on our failure.[12]

Critically thinking about diet theories and strategies requires that we ask three questions. First, we need to ask why people want to lose weight. If they are motivated by shame, the likelihood of success is minimal as shame cannot be healed by losing weight. In such cases a diet program may even do more harm than good. In fact, some of the best literature on shame and dieting, including the best seller *Overcoming Overeating*, suggests that the most important first step in creating a diet program is to decide not to diet.[13]

Second, we need to ask if diets work. Most people think diets work and it is the dieters who "don't work." However, any review of unbiased research literature not done by the diet industry leads to the conclusion that, in fact, diets don't work. Professor Steven Hawks of Brigham Young University says, "You would be hard pressed to review the dietary literature and conclude that you can give people a set of dietary guidelines or restrictions that they will be able to follow in the long term and manage their weight successfully."[14] Similarly, Professor Traci Mann of UCLA, after conducting a comprehensive analysis of thirty-one diet studies, concluded that most dieters would have been better off never dieting at all since the majority of them gained all their weight back and more.[15] In fact, if we could ask a person one question to help us predict whether they will gain weight it is this: Are you dieting? If diets were medicine, few would be helped, some would experience no change, and most would get sicker. Thus, it seems diets are bad medicine.

Finally, we need to inquire about the health implications associated with being overweight to better understand the need for dieting. While being overweight, in and of itself, is associated with identified health risks, eating certain foods, not moving or exercising, and having prior health issues may be more significant factors in people's health than weight alone. Further, one of the largest studies, conducted at Harvard University, found that the rate of heart disease and type II diabetes increase significantly with big weight fluctuations such as those experienced by yo-yo dieters.[16] Consequently, repeatedly losing weight and then gaining weight again, the most likely result of any diet program, may be more dangerous to our health than being overweight.

THE *DR. PHIL* SHOW

Dr. Phil has made dieting and weight loss the topic not only of many episodes of his television shows but also of his best-selling book, *The Ultimate Weight Solution: The 7 Keys to Weight Loss Freedom.* An episode of the *Dr. Phil* show focusing on brides to be who wanted to lose between forty and sixty pounds in the four months before their wedding provided good examples of some important issues regarding body image and dieting, and presented opportunities to consider various approaches to these issues.[17] Dr. Phil offered the brides to be a special incentive to lose weight: their ideal wedding dress in a size to match their ideal weight and a chance to win new wedding rings—what he called a wedding ring "upgrade." To illustrate the potential results, he had the dresses modeled by women who were significantly slimmer than his guests.

Perhaps the most haunting and painful aspect of the show was the intensity of self-hatred these women expressed toward their bodies, referring to themselves as *unattractive, disgusting, Amazonian, fat-ass,* and *sickening.* Clearly, the women thought their wedding day happiness was contingent on their weight loss. One said that she couldn't imagine her fiancé would find her attractive as she was and that she didn't want to look at her wedding pictures and "hate" the person she saw. Another remarked that she wanted to be proud of herself when she got married. A third said, "I want to be beautiful, not like this." A fourth indicated that she wouldn't be able to enjoy her wedding day as she was because she would be worrying about how she looked. A fifth had kept putting off her wedding day until she lost weight.

In addition, the women were filled with shame about their inability to lose weight, believing their personal failings had caused them to be over-weight and prevented them from losing the extra pounds. One woman had tried many diet programs, from Weight Watchers to Jenny Craig, but had been unsuccessful because, as she said, she "cheated." Another had tried to lose weight but couldn't. Still another had lost some weight but had been unable to lose more, reflecting a typical scenario as fewer than 10 percent of all dieters sustain weight loss. They all blamed themselves not their diets for their failure to lose weight, seeing themselves as lazy, stupid, pathological, rebellious, or lacking discipline. In short, they each thought, "Something is wrong with me."

The women's self-deprecation did not go unnoticed by Dr. Phil, who asked them to think about the negative effect this kind of self-criticism had on their self-images. He was clear that shame and guilt are not keys to successful dieting and that it was not necessary to lose weight to feel beautiful and have a positive self-image.

I agree with his response; it would have been a travesty to allow this kind of self-abuse to go unnoticed and unchallenged. Unfortunately, we have become so habituated to verbal self-abuse that we rarely challenge the assumptions of individuals who are being self-abusive in the same way we might intervene if we witnessed one person abusing another. However, ultimately Dr. Phil's main goal was to assist these women in losing weight rather than help them feel beautiful or loved.

The problem with Dr. Phil's approach is that he assumed these women were dieting for "good" reasons—to feel physically and emotionally better. However, when individuals instead work to lose weight because of shame, hoping to silence the voices of internal and external criticism, the odds of sustaining weight loss is low for the voices of self-criticism and feelings of shame about body image are likely to return after the wedding day. On the other hand, if the voices of self-criticism are silenced in a way that addresses the underlying psychological issues, resulting in the individuals feeling more beautiful and self-loving, then the reason for dieting at all may be called into question.

Consider the woman who said she wouldn't be able to enjoy her wedding day if she didn't become slimmer because she would be worrying about how she looked. If she worked to lose weight under this kind of duress, even though she might have a wedding day without judgment and shame she probably wouldn't have a future without them.

THE DIETERS' DILEMMA

One of the central dilemmas in understanding dieting and weight loss, what I call the "dieters' dilemma," is that genuinely questioning the reason for dieting means to consider not dieting at all, leaving people not knowing how to proceed. Psychotherapists Jane R. Hirschmann and Carol H. Munter, in their book *Overcoming Overeating*, show how giving up dieting is a necessary first step in building a healthy relationship with eating and our bodies. They propose that only after giving up dieting can we free ourselves from our eating habits and the never-ending cycle of criticizing ourselves, controlling ourselves, and then breaking free and binging. Hirschmann and Munter persuasively explain how we shouldn't be ruled by self-abuse and criticism—what motivates most people to diet.[18] Dr. Phil, like most people in the diet industry, never suggested that the brides to be consider not dieting. The dieting industry depends on people, particularly women, disliking their bodies, and trying to lose weight to remedy the situation. Dr. Phil's main goal was to help these women lose weight, not to help them feel free, beautiful, or love themselves. In fact, this episode of the *Dr. Phil* show expresses a double message implying that the women are beautiful the way they are but also that they could look better if they were thinner like the women modeling their ideal wedding dresses.

My own research has led to conclusions similar to those of Hirschmann and Munter: successful weight loss begins with building a new relationship with our bodies and our eating habits, one not based on the necessity of weight loss. This is the way to resolve the "dieters' dilemma." After working with twenty-two people, many over time, I have concluded that most people diet as a result of shame and self-hatred; shame and self-hatred rarely generate positive results; people's stories of pain and struggle regarding body image and eating patterns provide a window to understanding the motivation and meaning of their behavior; and learning to respond to internal and external criticism, and acknowledging the power and meaning in eating patterns, helps people love themselves and feel powerful and beautiful so they can live in better alignment with their true purposes.

The idea of loving ourselves, including loving our bodies, as a solution to helping people find a way of eating that nurtures and supports them is so unconventional that many people might question its effectiveness. We have come to believe so firmly that the way to well-being is to meet certain cultural standards, making appropriate changes to do so, that the notion of loving ourselves the way we are seems almost pathological rather than a worthy way to address the issue of dieting. But it is important to understand the significance of loving ourselves in this context.

Further, my research shows that we don't only diet for bad reasons, like shame and self-hatred, but we may eat for good reasons, motivated by self-love and coping mechanisms that provide support and useful psychological information. While Dr. Phil's approach assumed there was no deeper wisdom reflected in the eating or cheating of the women on his show, to try to change our eating habits it is imperative that we understand these urges. In my research, people never ate only as a result of laziness, stupidity, rebelliousness, or lack of discipline. The brides to be on the *Dr. Phil* show can also be seen as illustrating this view. The woman who said she would not enjoy her wedding day unless she lost weight mentioned that eating helped her control anxiety. While food may not be the best way of addressing her anxiety, this statement about her eating pattern reflects some real wisdom and self-awareness: "I am anxious. Eating somehow helps." If we tell such a woman simply to change her eating pattern, thus eliminating this coping strategy, we are not "listening to her eating" to understand important messages it is sending about her deeper motivations. Consequently she may manifest her anxiety in other ways or be unable to cope with her anxiety and repeat a vicious cycle of weight loss and gain. Instead, we need to discover the cause of her anxiety and find a way to help her address it.

Or consider the woman who kept putting off her wedding date because she hadn't lost sufficient weight. If we assume that her motivation for eating reflects self-love and wisdom rather than lack of discipline, then it is possible her eating may have been a message about a subconscious resistance to getting married that needs to be addressed before she proceeds. If we don't take the message of her eating seriously, she might simply continue to derail her wedding plans, keeping everyone, including herself, thinking that she is not getting married because she is not thin enough. As a result, she would keep hating her body and feeling ashamed of her inability to change.

Actually, it is quite common for issues around eating and dieting to be connected to relationship issues. Specifically, there are many cases where one partner is critical of their spouse's body features, weight, or eating habits. Feeling unloved and shamed by this puts the spouse in a double bind. If the spouse diets and loses weight, then they don't feel loved for who they really are; if the spouse doesn't diet and lose weight, they don't feel loved for who they are. The way out of this torturous paradoxical situation must include a real discussion between partners about how they feel and what they need to feel loved; dieting and losing weight is no substitute for this kind of intimate dialogue just as dieting and losing weight for the woman on the *Dr. Phil* show was no substitute for discovering the motivations behind her hesitation to get married.

A third woman on the *Dr. Phil* show, who felt like an Amazon as a child and was dieting so she wouldn't feel that way on her wedding day, also might illustrate how motivations for eating can reflect self-love or wisdom. She said she wanted to diet and lose weight so she wouldn't look or feel like an Amazon, but she did not really follow through with this intention. This woman's eating, like many women's, may be in rebellion against society's message that she needs to fit into a certain mold rather than being herself and thus provide information about her need for her own identity, which may actually have been reflected in her childhood feelings of being like an Amazon. In other words, while she might want to diet to avoid being like an Amazon, she may eat to express her Amazonian nature, or her individuality. In fact, she said she wanted to stand up straight and proud, and being Amazonian may be the fast track to attaining that goal.

Dr. Phil picked up on the double message of her behavior—that while she said she wanted to diet and lose weight she has not followed through with this intention. He challenged her, asking if she *really* wanted to lose weight. However, he didn't do this to discover and support the message of her eating; he did it as a way of pointing out her lack of commitment to losing weight. When she confessed that she "cheats," Dr. Phil again chided her by saying that she rebels against restrictions, ignoring her marvelously devilish smile as she made her confession. Dr. Phil's approach assumed there was no deeper wisdom or self-love expressed by her eating, and thus he not only sided with the consensus opinion that dieting is better than not dieting but also inadvertently sided against her Amazonian nature, which might symbolically reflect her authentic self.

Her story reminds me of a woman I worked with who had been told, since age five, that she was husky. She was a large, beautiful, intelligent, and powerful woman who had worked in the Fire Department, spent years in the military, and was now studying to be an EMT. Though she had tried to become smaller over years of feeling self-hatred and shame, nothing had helped her succeed. Her efforts had even led her, while in the military, to cover her thighs and belly with Preparation-H and wrap herself with Saran wrap overnight. One day in my office she told me how bad she felt being so big and how much she wanted to lose weight, commenting that her size was like a great weight on her that dragged her down. While I was tempted, like people in the diet industry, to help her get rid of some weight, I decided to see if wisdom and self-love motivated her eating pattern. I asked her to stand up and give me her hand, then pulled it until she indicated that I was beginning to drag her down the way she thought her weight did. However, rather than allowing herself to be dragged down, she fought back with a power many times my own. Finally, I asked, "Who are you that I can't drag you down?" "I am a bear," she replied as tears began streaming down her face. "I named my son Bjorn, which means bear, but before today I never knew why." This woman could not be dragged down in life. When something tried to stop her, whether it was people's criticism or standards set by employers, parents, or the culture, she always found a way to be bigger than those barriers and limitations. And now she had learned from me to love her bear nature—her size and the way she responded to challenge—rather than cling to the need to diet and lose weight.

The woman's story also raises the important issue of how societal double standards among genders regarding body size and weight are responsible for women's unnecessary self-consciousness, shame, and lack of opportunities. I witnessed another poignant example of such double standards in the 1980s as a consultant to a large healthcare organization. The group had twenty-six top executives, only one of whom was a woman, and she was leaving. The executive team charged me with helping them understand why they were having difficulty selecting women for the top level of the organization. I interviewed the team and also a woman currently applying for the job who was overweight by most standards. A number of the executives mentioned her weight and, when I asked them why they thought this was an issue, said that her inability to lose weight reflected her inability to be committed and responsible. However, there were men on the executive team equally large, and no one considered them ill equipped to do their jobs.

Our culture's double standards regarding gender and body image affect women's situations in various ways. For instance, regarding the woman who had been called an Amazon, if a man were called an Amazon it would likely be considered praise, but a woman being called an Amazon is criticism. Moreover, if a woman gains weight as the result of a natural female process such as pregnancy, she is still criticized, while if a man gains weight due to a physical condition he is less likely to be criticized. This perspective was illustrated on the *Dr. Phil* show when one woman said she had gained her weight when she was pregnant and her fiancé said he wanted the woman she used to be, without mentioning the crucial reason for her weight gain. In addition, her doctor had told her that she had a pretty face but a "meatball" body, shaming her in a way that causes many women to avoid doctors altogether. Such criticism, along with cultural double standards, drive women to diet unnecessarily and keep women and others from focusing on the deeper motivations behind eating.

CONCLUSION

It is evident that the prevalent myths and misinformation about dieting are widespread and misleading, making it imperative that we gain awareness of how potentially damaging they can be and share this information with friends and family, colleagues and community. Rebelling against societal voices of criticism regarding body image and eating patterns might be critical to development, especially women. In that case, sabotaging their own diet efforts and learning to "listen to their eating" may be acts of power, freedom, and self-love. I am suggesting something quite radical: that many individuals, especially women, do, in fact, resist self-hatred and defend themselves against society's attempts to shame them and impose negative self-images on them in an insidious manner *by gaining weight or not losing weight.* Even though gaining weight may not be the best way to stand up for oneself, it is certainly a powerful one. With all our cultural emphasis on the way people's bodies should look, perhaps it is inevitable that the fight takes place in the body. While this kind of protest song may seem irrational to some, my ears hear a beauty and power in it as well.

Dieting As an American Koan

Zen and the Art of Weight Loss

Some long ago when we were taught
That for whatever kind of puzzle you got
You just stick the right formula in
A solution for every fool.
—Indigo Girls

MILLIONS OF PEOPLE LOOK IN THE MIRROR or step on the bathroom scale and decide they want to lose weight, especially if they are anticipating an event that might lead to public criticism of their body size, like the brides in the episode of the *Dr. Phil* show discussed in the previous essay.[1] And billions of dollars are spent, along with countless lives haunted, trying to answer the question of how to lose weight. The most popular answer, and seemingly the most reasonable, is to go on a diet. Experts and nonexperts alike tell us, often for a hefty fee, to eat more fiber, cut down on sugar, eat less gluten, eat more vegetables, drink more water, reduce calorie intake, or eat less food more often. Another popular answer is to take a weight-loss supplement, anything from an appetite suppressant, such as Liporexall or Phenedrine, to a drug that helps burn fat, like DecaSlim and Lipofuze. Yet another answer is to focus on the ever-popular wide range of exercise programs.

The question is simple to ask; the answers are plentiful and logical. So it would seem that success should readily follow. But instead people try to lose weight and fail or repeatedly lose weight and gain weight in a process referred to as yo-yo dieting. After studying people's experience with diets, it is clear that the question of how to lose weight cannot simply be solved by logical action—eat less, exercise more—but is instead more like a koan, a question that confounds and defies comprehension until we awaken to a new understanding.

Koans, which derive from the Zen tradition, are questions, riddles, or paradoxes presented by a master to a student to perplex their rational mind and dislodge it from its habitual assumptions and thought patterns. The student could ponder a koan for months or even years, bringing answers to the master, who evaluates them and, unless the student has broken free from habitual patterns of thinking, refuses to accept them, then, after whacking the student with a teaching stick, sends the student away to contemplate further. For example, one traditional koan asks the student, "What is the sound of one hand clapping?" If the student answers logically, such as saying, "The sound is a kind of whoosh that occurs when the hand moves through the air," the master might reply, "Go back and meditate for six more months." However, if the student becomes frustrated and blurts out something like, "I don't know," the master might say, "Good, you're on your way." This is because an admission of not knowing can become the first step in shifting the student's mindset, or as one Zen master said, "You have to empty your cup before you can refill it."

Looking at the question of how to lose weight as a great American koan, it is clear that people have "meditated" on it for years, desperate to determine an answer. The dieter comes up with a plan, such as a fortified resolve to eat less and exercise more, but eventually returns to the bathroom scale, mirror, or low self-worth with a sense of failure if, despite their attempt, they have not changed their basic assumptions. Then an imaginary master takes out a teaching stick, whacks the dieter on their shoulder, and sends the dieter back to try a new approach. The dieter tries harder, just as students do with koans, but if again the dieter doesn't change some basic assumptions the same cycle will be repeated.

Consider the following scenario concerning an imaginary student and a Zen master. The student goes to the master and has a dialogue with him.

Student: Master, how can I lose weight?

Master: How do you *think* you can lose weight?

Student: I think I need to exercise more, count my calories, maybe take diet pills. I need more discipline; I need to stick with a program. If I were to go to Jenny Craig, go on the South Beach diet, or do the Atkins diet, I would have a program to follow.

Master: Very well. Do this and come back in three years.

Student: I've already tried these ideas for years; I'm coming to you for a new answer. Don't you have any wisdom to offer?

Master: Keep doing what you have been doing.

Student: You're no help; you're a fraud.

Master: Good. I can understand why you are frustrated and distrustful of me. There is just one thing that I don't understand.

Student: What is that?

Master: Why are you not distrustful of your diet strategies? Perhaps you *don't* need a diet, in which case find the way that is not about what and how much you eat.

In this scenario, the student begins to break free from habitual thought patterns and is thus able to entertain new possibilities.

SOME ANSWERS TO THE DIETING KOAN

Like the master suggests, are there approaches to the question of how to lose weight that don't involve what and how much we eat? Consider the situation of Audrey, a participant in my research study who is a single mother of two. She desperately wanted to lose weight but began eating more every time she even thought about starting a new diet. "It's crazy—I'm not even on the diet yet, and I'm hungry and snacking all the time. I decide to eat salad every day or drink more water, and the next moment I am snacking on foods I don't even like," she explained.

Audrey believed she needed to be more committed to her diets. Knowing this was her belief but that it hadn't worked for many years, I suspected it was not the answer to her koan. To go deeper, I engaged Audrey in a role play; I played the role of the person who thought she needed more discipline, and she played the role of the individual who ate more when she thought of dieting. We had the following conversation.

Me: You will eat salads every day; you will drink more water. You will do exactly what I say. No more excuses.

Audrey: I am going to find ways to rebel.

Me: No, you will do exactly what I say. Stay within this box. (I draw an imaginary box around her.)

Audrey: I am going to put my foot on the other side of that box. I want to show you I have a little power. I'll stick to your plan most of the time but not totally.

Me: But I made rules that will help you, and you must abide by them.

Audrey: I can't. I have to be able to say no.

Me: Saying no must be very important to you. So please explain to me the importance of your ability to say no.

Audrey: Saying no is something only for myself; it's putting my own two feet on the ground. It's not even why I say no that's important but just the ability to say it. It's more than a declaration of power; it shows I exist. I can't say no without repercussions at work because I can't afford to lose my job. I can't say no to my children's needs because I am the only one there. So the ability to say no in other situations is important for me to feel free, to feel I exist as an individual.

Audrey was a caring woman who, because of trying to be both a good employee and single parent, had no time left for herself. Believing she could not say no in almost every circumstance, she unconsciously set up a diet plan that she felt she should follow and then say no to, thereby asserting her power and individuality. Her dieting evidently had to do with more than actually losing weight. Subsequently, Audrey and I set up a new diet plan that incorporated learning to say no in other areas of her life—sometimes to her kids, to being a perfectionist about housecleaning, and to getting up early on weekends, all of which allowed her to take more time for herself. As a result of learning to say no in other areas of her life, Audrey didn't lose much weight, but she was happier and stopped putting herself on diets that led only to repeated weight loss and gain.

Further, consider the situation of Erica, who also found that her diet plan was not really about eating less. She gained weight during pregnancy with her first child, then tried to lose it but failed. Focusing on her calorie intake, she complained of a terrible habit of drinking Starbuck's caramel mocha lattes. Even though the nearest Starbucks was twenty minutes from her house, she still found time to make the drive even late at night, and spend the money to buy lattes—an expense her husband didn't approve of. She tried drinking more water, drinking fewer lattes, putting less sugar in them, and ordering them with skim milk, each of which was unsuccessful.

To determine what might be behind her obsession with these drinks, I handed her a plastic water bottle and asked her to imagine she was holding one of those magic elixirs. She grasped the water bottle and, closing her fingers firmly around it, said that she could feel how much she wanted it.

I then reached for the water bottle saying that I was going to take it away from her. I began pulling; she began pulling. She stood up; I stood up. We laughed at the absurdity of this struggle, which had somehow become more real than she had expected, as we had the following exchange.

Erica: I'm not letting go.

Me: Of what?

Erica: My happiness.

In this way it became clear what the lattes represented in her life and that her diet concerned more than the wish to lose weight.

Digging deeper, it was revealed that Erica had a job she didn't like and a controlling husband. She was intelligent and desired a career as a lawyer, but her husband was dismissive of her dream, wanting her to stay home and take care of their two children, believing that a mother should devote herself to her family not to personal ambitions. However, about a year later Erica grabbed her happiness: she left her husband, went back to school, and began working in a law firm. As a result of these life changes, she was not only happier but mysteriously lost the weight she hoped to lose. Doing what made her happy was her diet program. She discovered the answer to her koan by breaking her habitual assumptions about dieting.

Finally, consider the case of Kelley, who wanted to diet but was a hamburger connoisseur. She could not suppress her desire to eat hamburgers. She loved her hamburgers with everything—a big beef patty, bun, cheese, mustard, ketchup, mayonnaise, bacon, lettuce, tomato, and dill pickles. She was also very particular about how she wanted them prepared: cooked medium with garlic powder, seasoning salt, and diced egg mixed into the meat. She dieted by eliminating specific aspects of her hamburger such as the bun, the mayo, or the cheese. But she still craved what she called a "real" hamburger, one with the works.

To help Kelley get perspective on her habitual thinking—that limiting the quantity of hamburgers she ate and the accompanying ingredients was the key to her dieting—I asked her to convince me that she needed hamburgers with everything on them. We had the following conversation.

Me: Can't you go without cheese?

Kelley: It's not really a hamburger without cheese.

Me: Why ketchup, mustard, *and* mayonnaise?

Kelley: You need them all because together they create a special flavor.

Me: But certainly you don't need the bun; bread adds empty calories.

Kelley: It wouldn't be a sandwich without bread. It all has to be there! It is beautiful how you can get all those ingredients with so many colors on a round piece of bread.

Me: Tell me about having to have everything exactly the way you want.

Kelley: I never get to have exactly what I want. Never.

This exchange made it clear that fighting her hamburger hunger was not the answer to her koan. After her revelation that she had been an accommodator with regard to the needs of her parents and later her husband and children, Kelley and I set up a new diet program that began by allowing her to eat "doctored up" hamburgers whenever she desired as a way of practicing getting exactly what she wanted. Several weeks later she mysteriously began eating fewer hamburgers and talking to me more about all the ways she accommodated others in her life. The next step in her diet program was to paint some of the rooms in her house the colors she had wanted before being overruled by her family and to talk to them about going back to school to get her college degree.

For these women, breaking habitual patterns was the answer to their koans. Like most people, they believed that weight gain came from eating too much and not exercising enough. However, they discovered answers outside their habitual thinking about dieting, which led them to the real reasons behind their cravings for certain foods and beverages and their resistances to diet plans. Consequently, their real diets involved getting a new job, leaving a relationship, or taking more time for personal activities to achieve greater happiness.

CONCLUSION

Many people who struggle with how to lose weight—an American koan—might benefit from breaking their habitual thought patterns about dieting to discover the underlying reasons for their eating patterns, thus solving their koans in surprising ways according to the information they obtain. However, for people who have spent years facing dieting and weight loss problems, it is also important to realize that the dynamics underlying the struggles related to eating and body weight can be deep and powerful, requiring a large measure of mercy and even grace. Or as the *I Ching*, a noted Chinese source of wisdom, says, "No blame," since some koans take a lifetime or more to solve.

Can I Get a Witness?

Taking a Stand against Assaults on Body Image

> *It is a peculiar sensation, this double-consciousness,*
> *this sense of always looking at one's self through the eyes of others,*
> *of measuring one's soul by the tape of a world that*
> *looks on in amused contempt and pity.*
> —W. E. B. Du Bois

WHY DO PEOPLE, ESPECIALLY WOMEN, criticize their bodies so ruthlessly, expressing such self-hatred and shame when they look in the mirror? Practitioners of mainstream psychology, like Dr. Phil on his show, address this question as if individuals were the cause and therefore the solution to such suffering, implying that it is people's bodies and their lack of self-esteem that need to be changed. But this approach is like blaming the victim while keeping others free from responsibility. It ignores the role all people play in creating the cultural standards that cause so many individuals to criticize their bodies and focus on weight loss.

Consider the brides to be on the *Dr. Phil* show who felt they had to lose weight prior to their wedding days to avoid judgment and shame.[1] While anticipation of a wedding can elicit feelings of love and blessing, for these women it evoked anxiety and self-scrutiny provoked by conventional cultural standards of beauty. Dr. Phil encouraged their anxiety and self-scrutiny of their body images by offering to buy the women their ideal wedding dress in a size too small for them at their current weight. The message: It was their bodies that needed to be changed not the culture's narrow-minded and hurtful attitudes about body image.

People like the women on the *Dr. Phil* show are not born with a self-critical view but rather learned to see themselves through the eyes of others. W. E. B. Du Bois, referring to a similar predicament for African Americans seeing themselves through the lens of an oppressive and marginalizing culture, called this "double-consciousness."[2] The danger of double-consciousness is that it causes us to conform to an external standard created not out of truth, love, and justice but out of ignorance, fear, and contempt. The internal conflict that results can be demoralizing, if not devastating.

The facts are that our culture objectifies people by evaluating bodies according to superficial notions about beauty and attractiveness. This objectification of the body then leads to an internalized objectification so that we treat ourselves as objects of evaluation, manipulation, and commodification. This internalized objectification can be witnessed in the way people talk to themselves, using a voice that seems intelligent and motivated by self-improvement but, when examined more closely, is invariably condescending, gender biased, and uncompassionate. People, especially women, who experience internalized objectification, compared with those who do not, suffer greater shame,[3] more eating disorders,[4] reduced capacity to be in touch with their bodies,[5] decreased ability to perform cognitive tasks,[6] higher anxiety,[7] and less self-empowerment.[8]

These facts about our culture's objectification of people lead to some critical questions. For instance, why do we remain blind to the myriad forms of beauty? Have we come to believe there is an absolute, God-given standard of beauty? Have we simply become so accustomed to cruel judgments that seeing ourselves as other than beautiful has become a habit? Are we so lacking self-empowerment that we see our own beauty only when we receive approval from others, as if we were Sleeping Beauty waiting to be awakened by a prince? And if people like the women on the *Dr. Phil* show are being assaulted by such societal standards do they show so few signs of this because they have so little love for themselves that they no longer even acknowledge their injuries? This was apparently the case for a woman I worked with years ago who was a size zero but fretted about her "butt being still too big." She ate so little that she passed out several times at the gym because she exercised hard with no energy to burn. The only suffering she expressed was her inability to lose more weight; and while her parents encouraged her to eat more they were willfully blind to the violence right before their eyes.

To face our collective responsibility for such circumstances, we must bear witness to assaults on people's body image and the resulting suffering by learning to listen to what goes on inside people even when they do not speak out loud; noting their injuries even when they are denied; and responding with compassion and outrage, thereby taking a stand against these types of injuries.

Listening to people's internalized voices is not easy since we cannot hear their words. When individuals talk to themselves about body image, we don't witness them being verbally abused, even though this is precisely what tends to occur. However, if we listen to the internalized voices of our loved ones and ourselves speaking about body image, or read the words others have used to describe such experiences, we can get a good idea of how the self-abuse occurs. For example, phrases I have heard uttered by clients include: "You are fat, disgusting"; "Look at those arms, those breasts, those jowls"; "Food is evil and will make you fat and ugly"; "No one is ever going to want to be with you"; "Only weak people eat"; "You don't deserve anything"; "No one cares about you"; "You lazy stupid shit"; "I'm not going out with you like that"; and "Better to stay home, where people can't see you." One woman, while in my presence, looked at herself and said, "You ugly, stupid, worthless, fat bitch. What is wrong with you that you can't lose a few pounds?" with such ferocity that I was momentarily shocked, as if seeing the first flesh-and-blood image of war after thinking of war only in terms of strategies and statistics. Hearing these words so powerfully spoken gave me a good idea of what people say to themselves with internalized voices when they are unhappy with their bodies.

Many books and articles focus on such self-criticism. And numerous authors have done research as I did, by asking women what they say to themselves when they look in the mirror.[9]

To further grasp the damage of such self-criticism, we can imagine the brides to be on the *Dr. Phil* show parading before an examiner who, with red pen in hand, deducts points for their bodily "flaws," starting with the hair and ending with toenails, while simultaneously pronouncing the abusive assessments these women later hear in their heads. If we were to witness such a grotesque scene, certainly many of us would protest against the examiner's role and our hearts would go out to the women who were verbally abused. Awareness of what we were seeing and hearing would free us to respond appropriately, transforming our culture of innocence, collusion, and denial to one of healing.

CONCLUSION

It is time we offer more than diet advice and diet programs to help people with deeper psychological issues regarding body image. We should listen to their internalized criticism to understand the messages about cultural standards that are injuring them. We should also collectively share responsibility for the suffering people experience due to our cultural standards associated with body image. For starters, we can recognize that we are all witnesses to the suffering caused by cultural standards regarding body image: it is our eyes that do or do not see people's beauty; it is our criticisms that assault and injure them; it is our ears that can or cannot hear their suffering; and it is our voices that do or do not speak out in protest of cultural standards. Moving forward, we can then educate the ignorant about how cultural standards regarding body image injure people, take a stand against assaults on body image, and reach out with compassion to the millions who are being injured.

PART IV

ADDICTIONS AND OBSESSIONS

Substances As Allies

The Urge for Altered States

People say that what we're all seeking is a meaning for life.
I don't think that's what we're really seeking.
I think that what we're seeking is an experience of being alive.
—Joseph Campbell

A DDICTIONS ARE WOVEN INTO THE FABRIC of many social problems, including domestic violence, child abuse, theft, and drunk driving. While there is a logical imperative to eradicate this scourge, getting people to do so has proved extremely difficult. Research suggests that the effectiveness of treatment for addictions is not only limited, with even the best treatment programs reducing people's substance use only by about 50 percent,[1] but that motivating people to remain abstinent or in treatment has been a major hurdle. It appears that the reasons people use addictive substances are often more compelling than their desire to be free from the suffering and damage addictions cause. This is reflected in the following facts and statistics. According to Nora D. Volkow, M.D., director of the National Institute on Drug Abuse, about 75 to 80 percent of people who try to quit smoking relapse within six months.[2] Within one month after residential alcohol detoxification treatment, about 50 percent of patients relapse; about half of the remaining patients relapse after three months; and half of those who still abstain at three months relapse by six months. In their study on relapse rates, B.T. Jones and J. McMahon found that

108

after people had been discharged from a ten-day residential alcohol detoxification unit 51 percent relapsed by the end of one month and 72 percent relapsed by the end of three months.[3] Further, while Alcoholics Anonymous (AA) has done much to help people get off of drugs and alcohol, its ability to motivate people to sustain their efforts is also limited, reflected by the fact that of 100 individuals referred to AA, about 50 attend initially, about 25 still attend after three months, and only about 10 are still attending by the end of the second year.[4] Moreover, in therapeutic communities where patients and therapists live together, only about 7 to 26 percent of all admissions remain beyond one year.[5]

While some people suggest that it is the biochemical aspect of addiction that makes abstinence so difficult to sustain, getting people to make behavioral changes that are not complicated by biochemistry seems to be similarly difficult since less than 30 percent of people comply with doctors' recommendations to lose weight, exercise, or restrict their diets.[6] Considering the fact that about 20 percent of people can abstain from alcohol without any treatment, it is clear that our ability to motivate people to abstain from drugs and alcohol beyond their own readiness, willingness, and ability to do so on their own hardly competes with the powerful desires that fuel the use of these substances.[7]

These results beg the questions: "Why do people use and abuse substances?" and "What makes these reasons so compelling?" Mainstream thinking about these questions has offered little understanding, instead often blindly adopting an attitude of moral contempt toward people with addictions, seeing them as irresponsible, weak, and having a problem that "other people" have, even though most people have various addictive tendencies. Further, we have learned to treat addictions like malignant tumors—things to be removed, as if their expression has no meaning for the person or the culture. Mainstream psychology hasn't gone much further in demonstrating an understanding of the powerful motivations that fuel addictions. Typical reasons found in magazines and books, as well as on Internet sites, include the avoidance of unwanted feelings, self-medication due to stress, dealing with boredom, curiosity, or the desire to feel good—reasons that are devoid of critical thinking and reflect preconceived notions about substance use.[8]

This kind of simplistic thinking is even taught in university textbooks, including the popular *Drugs in Perspective: Causes, Assessment, Family, Prevention, Intervention, and Treatment* by Richard Fields, the textbook I used in a class I taught on addictions and dependencies. At the beginning of Fields's text, he writes that "all people consciously or subconsciously alter their state of consciousness,"[9] suggesting that they do so to increase their ability to feel pleasure; make friends; defy authority; deepen their sexual experiences, religious insights, or appreciation of beauty; and better understand themselves and others. In further support of the legitimacy and power of these motivations, Fields states that the drive to alter consciousness is "innate" and "one of several natural human drives such as hunger, thirst, and the drive to survive, as well as the sex drive with the goal of procreation."[10] However, as the book proceeds Fields leaves this basic understanding behind, replacing it with simplistic and moralistic explanations that do not exemplify a deep understanding of people's motivations or offer empirical knowledge from study and experience. These latter explanations include the notion that people have addictions because they are "passive procrastinators and conflict avoiders" or because they are "in search of a magic pill or cure for pain." He finally abandons deeper psychological understanding when he asserts that the "reason for using drugs/alcohol is often an attempt to alleviate feelings of boredom, melancholia, and sadness, fatigue or something to break up the monotony of everyday activities."[11] Typical of mainstream psychological thinking,

Fields ignores motivations based on a broader perspective, such as religious experiences, sexual experiences, or social needs, and he fails to address the deeper meaning and motivations that fuel addictions, instead relying on popular projections like stress reduction or alleviation of the boredom and monotony of mundane daily life. Focusing on such motivations adds little to our understanding of people's addictions or how to improve relapse rates.

In addition, mainstream psychology, with its agenda of holding individuals personally responsible and treating them, ignores social factors that play roles in the addictive process, including the fact that certain individuals and social groups suffer disproportionally from addiction to particular substances. Reasons for addiction like boredom, curiosity, stress reduction, or the desire to feel good do not address people's specific backgrounds or social conditions. This view ignores the fact that when people have unmet needs, some of which are caused by mainstream culture's biases, they are more likely to achieve fulfillment of those needs in ways that are less sanctioned and more disturbing.

THE *DR. PHIL* SHOW

Several episodes of the *Dr. Phil* show have concentrated on individuals with addictions, including people who drank too much or took too many painkillers or other substances. Dr. Phil treats such addictions very seriously, aware of their harmful impact on people's lives and the difficulties in treating them because of how deeply addictions take root. He uses the power of his persuasive arguments and authority to get people with addictions to acknowledge their need for help and to undergo treatment, often involving a lengthy stay at a rehabilitation facility. He also has what one of my teachers called an excellent "bullshit detector" when he hears people make excuses or otherwise deny or minimize their problem. In addition, he analyzes addictions with an eye toward the reasons people use substances, telling the guests on his show that they have to acknowledge the purpose of their addictions, which, at least for the purposes he identifies, are consistent with mainstream psychological thinking.

An episode of the *Dr. Phil* show provided an example of mainstream thinking concerning addictions.[12] On that show, Dr. Phil counseled two guests: one woman addicted to alcohol and another addicted to smoking cigarettes. Speaking to the woman addicted to alcohol, he suggested that the reason she drank was because it calmed her, eliminated her anxiety, or numbed her pain then asked, "Alcohol is a coping mechanism for you, correct?" After the smoker acknowledged that she didn't handle stress well, Dr. Phil said, "We need to replace one behavior with another," offering alternative ways to relax, including breathing exercises. He believed that she smoked to "ward off anxiety."

While it is reasonable to surmise that addressing motivations for addictions in these ways increases the effectiveness of efforts to break the addictive cycle, like mainstream psychological thinking the motivations Dr. Phil suggested were chosen from a narrow range of possibilities. While people regularly need coping strategies to deal with stress in their lives, there are often deeper and more potent subtexts to people's addiction stories.

ALTERNATIVE APPROACHES TO ADDICTIONS

Depth psychology, as explicated by Carl Jung and his successors, provides a different lens through which to view addictions and the motivations that fuel them. Depth psychology predicts that whenever we view something as an enemy with no redeemable characteristics, as mainstream psychology often does with addictions, we easily fall prey to projections, rush to judgment, and ignore its meaning and message. Like the process-oriented psychology of Dr. Arnold Mindell, depth psychology proceeds with the understanding that behind people's use and abuse of substances, from alcohol and methamphetamines to food and prescribed medications, is the desire to access altered states of consciousness, often to meet needs that our ordinary consciousness forbids.

I have affirmed this insight over many years by exploring past and current addictions with clients and with students in my university undergraduate class called Addictions and Dependencies. For example, I worked with an African American woman in her mid-fifties who had a history of cocaine addiction. While she wasn't using cocaine at the time, she had for a significant portion of her late adolescent and adult life. She said she had used cocaine because it was the only thing that had made her feel better. "In what way did you feel better?" I asked. She said cocaine had helped her forget how depressed she felt about her hard life. Wanting to dig deeper, beyond her ideas and into her actual experience, I asked her to recall more specifically what she had felt like when using cocaine. She sat up in her chair, and a strong and strident look appeared on her face. After becoming aware of her posture and appearance, she realized, for the first time, that using cocaine had enabled her to feel a sense of power, something she had never felt growing up poor, female, black, and in an abusive household. While she had believed her attraction to cocaine was to forget her pain, she now knew that it had actually helped her feel powerful and nearly invulnerable.

Another individual with whom I worked, a man in his late teens, living with his parents and hooked on hallucinogens, told me that he used these substances because his and his parents' lifestyle were boring. He would leave his parents' house, walk up a small hill just minutes away, take LSD or psilocybin mushrooms, and "just sit there." "What do you do when you sit there?" I asked. He said he thought about life. By exploring his motivation in this manner, I eventually learned that he was quite contemplative and interested in contemporary philosophical ideas, an interest at odds with his family's view that focusing on utilitarian things was the basis for success.

I also worked with an evangelical Christian who was ashamed to admit that he couldn't stop using marijuana, seeing his addiction as reflecting a weakness and lack of faith. To explore his motivation, I asked him to talk about his experience when using marijuana. He said he fixed on the glow at the end of the marijuana joint as his friends inhaled, saying, "It was like a candle," and described the warm yellow light he saw in his friends' faces. As he spoke, he teared up, the muscles on his face softened, and he elaborated on the love he had for his friends. Through these observations, I learned that it was not his lack of faith that motivated his abuse of marijuana but a desire for the light of friendship and community.

Another woman in her mid-fifties, small in stature, and even smaller in her sense of power in the world, loved to drink with her husband, saying it was a way to relax together. But since her husband had heart disease and high cholesterol and couldn't drink with her, they decided to smoke marijuana to enjoy a "little high" every so often. When I asked her what it was like, she said she hadn't really felt anything, but her husband had gotten quite stoned. "How do you know?" I asked. "He looked smaller," she said, an explanation that made me laugh. Her perceptions clearly reflected that her motivation for smoking marijuana had been to feel bigger and freer rather than to address her boredom or cope with stress.

These stories all reflect an essential truth concerning perceptions about addictions. Most people make up explanations about why they use certain substances that are not at all connected to the experiences they have using those substances. For example, the African American woman believed she used cocaine to feel less depressed about her hard life, but her actual experience using cocaine more clearly reflected the powerlessness she felt in her life and the sense of power she felt while using it. Similarly, the young man believed his use of hallucinogens was a response to boredom, but his experience using drugs revealed that it had more to do with his love of philosophical contemplation and a desire for a deeper inner life, a direction his parents did not approve of. The evangelical Christian man who used marijuana thought he did so because his will and faith were weak, but his actual experience of using drugs revealed he was hungry for the glow of friendship and sense of community.

These people had created armchair explanations of their substance use that appealed to mainstream culture and therefore were rarely questioned by others—reasons not grounded in their actual life experiences. The real reasons for their substance use had more to do with unrecognized inner needs and states of mind independent of their explanations. Their explanations reduced their powerful personal needs to psychological explanations they had likely learned from external sources, such as through friends, the media, and popular psychology expressed in books, magazines, or on the Internet. Consequently, because these individuals did not connect their addictions with deep personal needs, they treated themselves as if they needed correction, ignorant of the fact that they were searching for lives of greater meaning, power, and fulfillment—lives closer to their true natures.

One powerful firsthand experience I had of connecting an individual's addiction to a deep personal need underscored my belief that often the addictions of individuals reflect their search for lives of greater meaning and fulfillment. A female client wanted to quit smoking as she was afraid of its dangers since she had had several nonmalignant tumors and her mother and grandmother, both smokers, had died of lung cancer. To discover the deeper reasons for her smoking habit, I asked the woman about the rituals she engaged in and the state of mind she experienced while smoking. She told me that she lit her first cigarette of the day as she turned onto the highway in the morning while driving to work. She added that she didn't like her work, saying, "It is so impersonal," as if she were just a cog in a wheel. In actuality, not only did her job not foster deep relationships but she herself found intimacy difficult.

Next, wanting to know her actual experience instead of her ideas about her experience, I asked her to imagine smoking with me and to show me what she did. To do this, we created an imaginary car in my office with two chairs next to each other representing the front seats, and two more behind us representing the back seats. She was in the "driver's seat," while I was in the "passenger's seat." Two pens represented a couple of Winston Lights, one in her hand, one in mine.

"Let's smoke," I said, putting my pen to my mouth. She smiled and puckered up her lips around the pen, pulling imaginary smoke into her mouth and inhaling deeply.

"Tell me what you just did," I said.

"I inhaled," she answered.

"You inhaled awfully deeply. Do it again and describe very carefully what you are doing," I encouraged her.

"I am taking it in as deeply as I can," she replied.

"OK," I said, "then what happens?" Again she drew in imaginary smoke and then, to my surprise, did not exhale right away but held her breath.

"That was a long pause you took before exhaling. Can you tell me what you were doing then?" I asked.

After doing it a couple of more times quietly and attentively, she said, thumping on her chest, "I am waiting until I can feel it right here."

"OK, show me what happens next," I told her. She blew out a smooth, steady, forceful stream of imaginary smoke from between her pursed lips, making an audible blowing sound.

"Tell me what you were doing," I said.

"I was giving it back, letting out what is in me," she confided, again thumping her chest.

Focusing more on the ritual of her smoking, I urged, "Explain to me more about taking the smoke in deeply, holding it until you can really feel it in your chest, and then letting out what is in you."

Then she began to sob, saying, "Having someone really take me in, really listen to me, really feel me and then speak from their heart is the essence of life. I want that; I want to give that. It's what makes life worth living."

From her simple announcement "It's what makes life worth living," it was clear to see that the threat of illness or a shortened life could not compete with the power of the incentive that fueled her desire: she wanted to share with others deeply, from the heart. Smoking a cigarette the way she did gave her an experience of being alive, of feeling the nature of her own life force flowing through her veins and psyche. I realized that helping this woman quit, or at least decrease her smoking, would mean assisting her not only with a plan to resist cigarettes but also with a method for deepening her relationships. She had to build the skills to listen more intently, empathize more with others, and courageously ask people to speak more from their hearts. It took months for her to choose friends with whom she could be more intimate and years to leave her job and begin working for an organization more interested in her human resource skills, but at least the information she had received through exploring her motivation for smoking eventually became the basis for a more fulfilling life.

If we were to think like mainstream psychologists, we would have seen this woman as stressed, depressed, bored with her relationships, trying to cope with a job that wasn't satisfying, and experiencing anxiety about her health due to her years of smoking. But none of these issues was really her main motivation for smoking; in fact, I have rarely found these "usual suspects" to be anyone's motivation for addiction. Getting to the deeper reasons people use and abuse substances requires thinking outside the box of mainstream psychology, momentarily suspending our judgments and our armchair explanations, and believing that what people are doing reflects more meaningful needs and desires.

CONCLUSION

We express our natures and aliveness in myriad ways, yet they are often wrapped in culturally acceptable forms and limited by our capacities, degree of courage, and knowledge of ourselves. While these limits can be like the cement we walk upon fostering community and the easy flow of commerce, they can also take the form of unfulfilling jobs, beliefs that cramp and cripple us, or barriers to our creativity and development. When this is the case, our natures find circuitous paths through the cement toward our authentic selves and genuine life purposes. Sometimes these paths can lead us to powerful addictions.

One of my teachers, Dr. Max Schupbach, said that when individuals can't find their way home they usually find a hotel that reminds them of home. And sometimes they will even forget they are not home or be too scared to stray from a place that feels like home for fear that their lives will get lost. Addictions are a hotel; they are not home but can remind people of home so powerfully that they won't easily abandon them without knowing where their real home is and how to get there.

Making Me Over

Obsessing about Obsessions

I am circling around God, around the ancient tower,
and I have been circling for a thousand years,
and I still don't know if I am a falcon, or a storm, or a great song.
—Rainer Maria Rilke

O BSESSIONS CAPTURE OUR COLLECTIVE IMAGINATION because, despite the apparent irrationality of obsessed people, most of us have been obsessed with something at some point in our lives. One of the major obsessions people have in our mainstream culture is with celebrities; many Americans emulate celebrities and look to them for standards of beauty and success. Obsessions with celebrities reach the danger point, however, when people's devotion to the rich and famous leads them to make major life decisions to imitate them, subjecting themselves to countless surgeries or burning holes in their wallets purchasing clothes and accoutrements to fill up their psychic lives with dreams untouched by any sense of reality.

The approach of mainstream psychology to obsessions focuses on oversimplified explanations of the motivations propelling them, such as people's irrationality or low self-esteem, while ignoring people's deeper needs symbolically expressed in their obsessive behaviors. It tries to assert a Dr. Phil-type question such as "What are you thinking?" or "How's that working for you?" into a system that clearly defies such logic. In this way, mainstream psychology works to restore reason, normalcy, and functionality in people with obsessions by helping them reassert control over themselves and their lives.

THE *DR. PHIL* SHOW

An episode of the *Dr. Phil* show provided good examples of how mainstream psychology understands and deals with obsessions.[1] One of Dr. Phil's guests was a woman whose room was filled with pictures of Brad Pitt, a movie star known for his attractiveness. She had spent countless hours talking to her children about how wonderful Brad Pitt was and how she planned to marry him and live happily ever after. Her children, disturbed by her behavior, had written to Dr. Phil for help. Another guest was a woman who wanted to look like Jessica Simpson, a recording artist and television personality also known for her conventionally attractive appearance. This woman wanted to be like one of the guests on the television show *The Swan,* which portrays people getting radical makeovers to transform their physical appearances through physical exercise, dental and orthodontic care, and plastic surgery. She had surgically altered her appearance to achieve her goal, had bought the same clothes Simpson wore, kept up on all the news about Simpson, and stared reverently at pictures of her.

Dr. Phil created the impression that this woman's obsession was ridiculous, leaving his audience shaking their heads in disbelief, self-assured that they were more enlightened than her. However, while this show's topic was presented in a lighter manner than others Dr. Phil has addressed, these women's obsessions about celebrities clearly had a darker side. Most obviously, these women were making ill-advised financial decisions in pursuit of vicarious emulation; but on a deeper level, as Dr. Phil pointed out, the women had underlying psychic pains and suffering, such as low self-esteem, driving their obsessions.

Dr. Phil counseled these women with his usual formidable logic, challenging their irrational thinking and irresponsible behavior, including their large expenditures on the right clothes and the surgical reshaping of their bodies. He tried to call their attention to their delusional perspectives, for example, by asking the woman who was obsessed with Brad Pitt, "What if this doesn't happen?" He understood their obsessions to be manifestations of their fragile self-esteem, which prevented them from seeing their own beauty and worth. Addressing the Jessica Simpson wannabe, Dr. Phil pointed out that while she wanted to be "drop-dead gorgeous," she didn't feel good looking at herself. In an effort to boost her self-esteem, Dr. Phil asked, "What *is* good about you?" causing her to access painful feelings about herself and cry.

In counseling these women and educating his audience, Dr. Phil revealed that the underside of our culture's obsession with celebrities is low self-esteem—that the surgeon's steel applied to bodies to remake them in the image of others is covering over wounds of low self-esteem with scar tissue. However, in focusing generally on low self-esteem being the motivation for these women's obsessions, he failed to look for specific clues about the underlying needs hidden in their rituals and projections.

LIMITATIONS OF MAINSTREAM PSYCHOLOGY'S APPROACH TO OBSESSIONS

Mainstream psychology's tendency to diagnose people with obsessions, such as those who use vast resources to look like celebrities, as having low self-esteem and to suggest that they can be treated by a strong dose of sound reason and a booster shot of self-esteem warrants some critical thinking. Mainstream psychology conceives of self-esteem as a basic quality of people's makeup, as if it can be measured like the oil level in our cars by merely pulling out our dipsticks and seeing whether our self-esteem tank is high or low. Treatment then follows measurement—if someone's self-esteem is too low, they are advised to boost it, perhaps by practicing positive affirmations or self-appreciation.

However, there are several drawbacks to thinking of self-esteem in such a manner. First, it leads to oversimplification that prevents deeper investigation. It takes the fantasies and particulars of people's patterns of behavior (one person wants a certain handbag, chin, eyebrow, or manner of speaking; others wash their hands dozens of times a day, check their phone for messages every five minutes, or keep looking in the mirror for wrinkles or gray hair) and dismisses their nuances, power, and meaning. Thus when Dr. Phil treats the woman obsessed with being like Jessica Simpson as if she needs her self-esteem boosted, he never delves into the needs that lie behind her fixation on Jessica Simpson and the forces that work against her satisfying those needs. To pursue such a deeper under-standing, it would be necessary to ask the woman what she imagined it would be like to be Jessica Simpson. Her answers might include, "People would listen to what I have to say," "I would stop criticizing myself," or "I would no longer be lonely." Each response would provide a meaningfully different view of the dynamic underlying her obsession. Once we have identified her specific needs and desires, we would then begin an inquiry into the obstacles that impede their attainment—that prevent her from being heard, sustain her self-criticism, or contribute to her feeling lonely. Such information would lead to a more accurate understanding of the factors behind her obsession and suggest more individualized interventions.

For example, the three possible underlying needs fueling her obses-sion should be addressed by three different interventions rather than just focusing on her low self-esteem. If her need were to be listened to, it might require helping her develop more courage, power, and voice in the outer world.

In addition, countering the forces that thwart the satisfaction of this need might necessitate encouraging her to stand up against cultural forces that make it hard for women to express their authority. If her need were to be free from self-criticism, it might require teaching her to become more aware of the effects of such self-criticism and how to respond to it. If we worked to boost her self-esteem without helping her learn to respond to self-criticism, her self-esteem would be repeatedly raised but then lowered without any sustainable change. It would be like telling a person who was being bullied that they didn't deserve it without helping them learn to deal with the bully. If her need were to address her loneliness, it might necessitate teaching her how to meet people and the factors making it difficult for her to do so, or to flourish living alone in a world that values coupling over being single, especially for women. Focusing only on self-esteem would fail to help the woman become more aware of the complex underlying needs that have led to her obsession with Jessica Simpson. Addressing such aspects is especially critical in cases involving women's obsessions with their appearance because mainstream culture's propensity to connect women's worth to physical beauty makes it more likely that needs other than the need to feel attractive—such as the need to express intelligence, power, or moral authority—will get channeled into concerns with appearance. When this happens, a focus on self-esteem will not only overlook these underlying needs and the forces that thwart their satisfaction but lead to interventions that dismiss the diversity of women's strengths, abilities, and gifts—interventions that can easily become patronizing.

In addition, the tendency to see obsessions primarily in terms of low self-esteem pathologizes people, treating them as if their obsessions are caused by an underlying illness rather than a lack of self-knowledge about potential unmet needs and the inability to defend themselves against being judged or marginalized. A diagnosis of low self-esteem sends the message that people act obsessively because something is wrong with them, that if people felt better about themselves they would no longer cling to false idols and their obsessions would disappear like flu symptoms—a message that dismisses the creativity and resourcefulness of the psyche. By contrast, viewing obsessions as reflecting meaningful but perhaps hidden needs sends the message that people have powerful desires they may be unaware of and which may need more support as well as more protection from harsh and unfair inner and outer criticism.

The differential impact of these two messages cannot be overstated. The first message can increase the shame people feel by giving them one more reason to think they are unworthy, amplifying their low self-esteem, while the second message can lead to self-knowledge of their needs and worthiness to be protected, boosting their self-esteem and empowering them. Thus paradoxically, focusing on the underlying meaning of obsessions builds people's awareness of their needs and helps them follow their unique life paths, ridding them of those very symptoms that lead others to diagnose them as having low self-esteem in the first place, while diagnosing obsessed people with low self-esteem diverts attention from the underlying dynamics crucial to helping them make sustainable changes while inadvertently causing them to feel less well about themselves.

PROCESS-ORIENTED PSYCHOLOGY'S APPROACH TO OBSESSIONS

In contrast to mainstream psychology, process-oriented psychology views obsessions neither as a reflection of irrationality nor as the result of low self-esteem. Instead, it sees obsessions as manifestations of deferred needs and unlived dreams that, given the psyche's capacity for creativity, manifest in symbolic forms. While process-oriented psychology acknowledges people's need to have a measure of control over themselves and their lives, it also recognizes that extreme patterns of behavior are fueled by meaning-ful needs and desires not being fulfilled in the course of people's "normal" lives; that their return to normalcy is often unsustainable; and that gestat-ing in the destabilization brought about by obsessions are possibilities for more authentic lives. Furthermore, process-oriented psychology recognizes that the unfulfilled needs that fuel obsessions are rarely conscious and that consequently individuals with obsessions frequently are unaware of the deeper motivations for their extreme behavior. The fact that these needs are usually unconscious almost guarantees that the individuals will try to meet them in ways that are indirect and irrational rather than transforming. Finally, this approach recognizes that there are great and unyielding powers behind obsessions, but instead of fighting these powers, as mainstream psychology does, it engages with them. This necessitates doing something that mainstream psychology avoids—temporarily forgoing efforts to encour-age obsessed individuals to reassert normalcy and instead delve into their shadows, where the deeper motivations and meanings of their obsessions lie.

Such a journey into the shadow world, beneath the world of logic and reason, was beautifully allegorized in the 1991 thriller *The Silence of the Lambs*. The movie revolves around a budding FBI agent, appropri-ately named Starling, and her pursuit of a serial killer, a man obsessed with becoming a woman. The movie portrays the senior FBI agents from whom Starling is supposed to learn as skillful and logical but having little psychological understanding of serial killers. The character with the psy-chological understanding necessary to mentor Starling—Dr. Hannibal Lecter—is himself not only a serial killer but also a brilliant psychiatrist at home in psychological territory. Lecter counsels Starling to look beneath the surface of the serial killer's actions for the deeper needs powering his obsession. In one conversation, Lecter tells Starling, "Of each particular thing, ask, What is its nature? What does he do?" Starling, still focused on the killer's surface actions, answers, "He kills women." Lecter, pushing her further, replies, "No, that is incidental. . . . What needs does he serve?" Seeing that Starling is stuck in her conventional way of thinking, Lecter answers, "He covets," explaining that it is upon the objects or people we covet that we project our deepest needs. Dr. Lecter is not fooled by the surface actions of obsessed people but instead knows that at the root of their obsessions are powerful needs. The movie clearly teaches that to correctly understand obsessions and transform them, we must not get rid of them but instead delve into obsessed people's shadows to unravel their tangled meanings.

Process-oriented psychology's approach seeks to discover the hidden meanings in people's obsessions by focusing on aspects of their behavior and their feelings about it. Pursuing such meanings requires temporarily suspending mainstream psychology's tools—the demand for rationality and its reliance on the scalpel of confrontation, which is often accompanied by an attitude of contempt. This approach is akin to the one Dr. Lecter teaches Starling, identifying and understanding the particulars of people's obsessions and offering new directions for intervention and change.

People's obsessions are fueled by powerful needs and forces that thwart the satisfaction of those needs, and when these needs and forces are not evident obsessive behavior can seem irrational and meaningless, having no clear direction. In other words, the way some people sculpt their bodies is informed by the intelligence of a true purpose, and forces thwarting that purpose are often invisible to those who do not use the right approach to its discovery. To help students in my Addictions and Dependencies class explore this way of thinking, I facilitated the following demonstration. I asked one student to imagine that something he deeply wanted was in one corner of the room and to walk in that direction as if he were trying to reach it, while the rest of the class made detailed observations. Without hesitation, the student walked in a straight line to the specified spot in the room. Next, I asked him to do the same thing while I tried to prevent him from reaching his destination. After these actions had been repeated several times, the class observed that the student reacted in a variety of ways to my attempt to block him, such as altering his course to get around me, trying to push me aside, and stopping and looking down as if he had no idea how to proceed. However, regardless of these actions, one thing remained constant: the student's behavior appeared meaningful in contrast to how it would have appeared if I had been invisible—namely, irrational and purposeless. This demonstration helped the students understand obsessive behavior as reflective of underlying needs.

The key to what lies behind an obsession is usually embedded in the story being told through ritualized behaviors, which often involves unidentified desires that meet with powerful resistance from disapproving family members, rigid cultural norms, or self-criticism. Consider, for example, the story of a female client whose obsession was being naked with others. Having learned to suppress her feelings, she had resorted to either talking to people about being naked or finding permissible outlets for her obsession like going to public hot tubs and saunas. She came to me for help because many men were, not surprisingly, misunderstanding her intentions. At first, not knowing about her obsession I felt uncomfortable when she initially spoke about how she enjoyed being naked at a recent excursion to a local health spa with hot tubs. I sought the counsel of my supervisor, who saw her obsessive behavior as a symbolic attempt to "get naked" and suggested that I ask her to really "get naked" by encouraging her to share her deepest feelings and secrets. Interestingly, this approach elicited all the awkward and self-protective behaviors that people typically demonstrate with regard to being seen physically naked by strangers.

As our work progressed, I learned that the woman was essentially invisible to her parents, who never spoke to her about her feelings or needs. Lacking this outlet for self-expression and following the culturally sanctioned path of exploiting her physical attractiveness with her peers, she created tensions with other girls her age and attracted boys who were interested in her sexually, but she had no genuine friends. Her obsession with being naked was not a manifestation of her low self-esteem but an expression of a deep unconscious longing for friendship, a need that was made more complicated by the way she had learned, as an attractive woman, to reach out to people. Over the weeks, we explored her shyness about letting people get to know her and how she could do this in a way that was slow and careful enough to feel safe. Her need to deeply connect with people manifested unconsciously by revealing and talking about her naked body, which ironically left her also unconscious of her natural shyness. In becoming more aware of her deeper needs for true friendship, she became more fulfilled and discovered her natural impulse to set boundaries for herself without anyone challenging or shaming her to do so. If I had focused on this woman's low self-esteem instead of the constrained system in which she lived, I would have missed the more profound intelligence that informed her behavior, leaving her still unaware of her need for friendship and how to fulfill it.

Using low self-esteem as a diagnosis for obsessions without understanding how obsessions reflect hidden needs almost never results in helping people deal with their obsessions because it ignores the underlying dynamics. Instead, we are better able to help people with obsessions by assuming that the most disturbing details about their behaviors are actually clues about what is important to the individual's personal fulfillment and by being aware that obsessions often occur as a result of specific needs as well as forces obstructing their fulfillment. In addition, it can be useful in identifying the attitudes, values, individuals, groups, or institutions that may be obstructing the fulfillment of their needs, and help the person develop the internal and external resources required to overcome these forces, such as challenging societal norms or believing in oneself despite adversity, and summoning sufficient courage.

CONCLUSION

Mainstream psychology has influenced our collective thinking about how to deal with obsessions, leading us to uncritically accept the theory that our obsessions arise because something is wrong with us—from irrationality to low self-esteem—an attitude that discredits our unacknowledged needs, extraordinary powers, and complexity. Even when people with obsessions are diagnosed as having low self-esteem and their self-esteem is boosted, this approach leaves them unaware of their true needs, creating a glass ceiling that limits the heights to which their self-esteem can ultimately reach. The theory that obsessions arise because of low self-esteem or some pathology convinces people that they are not psychologically sound or intelligent enough to understand and fulfill their deepest needs, actually diminishes their self-esteem by not acknowledging the intelligence reflected in the details of their behavior.

By contrast, obsessions can be viewed as manifestations of deferred needs and unlived dreams that, given the psyche's capacity for creativity, manifest in symbolic forms. From this perspective, people's attempts to boost self-esteem fail because they do not address the needs and dreams that fuel obsessions. Instead, we must learn to see people's obsessions as reflecting neither sickness nor deficiency but rather as powerful needs important to being their authentic selves and using their creative capacity to express these needs through symbols in our environment, such as celebrities. Too often people are told that their deepest needs and dreams are not rational, moral, or achievable, while what they really need is sufficient understanding and support to remain authentic and fulfill their needs and dreams.

PART V

DIVERSITY

All Together Now
Appreciating Family Diversity

The older I get, the more I realize that it is the differences in me
that make me somebody who's worth knowing; it's the differences in me
that gives me the ability to go out and influence my world.
—Wandering Grace, It Gets Better Project

D IVERSITY IS NOT JUST A SOCIETAL PHENOMENON; it's also a family reality, especially in today's world of increased possibilities and choices. In fact, many individuals get their first education in cultural diversity from observing how their families deal with diversity within the family. We know that society is divided into subgroups, each with its own values, perspectives, and communication styles. The differing attributes of subgroups promote survival, success, and a sense of belonging, while they enrich society by providing a wider range of possibilities in life. However, subgroup differences are also the basis for a ranking system within society and thus the distribution of power and authority, praise and privilege. One subgroup becoming more powerful than others causes marginalization of the nondominant subgroups. Families can also be divided into subgroups with different values, perspectives, and communication styles, even if a subgroup consists of only one individual. And, as in society, certain subgroups within families are more dominant while others are marginalized.

The study of societal and family diversity reveals three key psychological principles underlying the pain and suffering of marginalized subgroups.

First, they become targets for the projections of the dominant subgroup; rather than being seen objectively, they are identified with qualities that either threaten or offend that subgroup, allowing it to disown these qualities. The projections often include negative qualities, such as irresponsibility, dirtiness, moral inferiority, intellectual inferiority, and ugliness. Second, they are pathologized—that is, viewed as sick or inadequate and in need of treatment, correction, or conversion—or worse, seen as harmful to society rather than as part of the health and wholeness of the culture at large. Finally, they are devalued by the dominant subgroup rather than being appreciated for their wisdom, beauty, or contributions to the society. As a result of these dynamics of societal and family diversity, marginalized subgroups commonly experience less economic success and social acceptance; greater psychological pain, shame, and self-hatred; and an increased incidence of violence.

Mainstream psychology's approach to family diversity presents several problems. When one or more family members do not exhibit the values, perspective, and communication style of the dominant family subgroup, practitioners of mainstream psychology frequently side with the dominant subgroup, amplifying the marginalization and suffering of the nondominant family members and obstructing the healing and wholeness of the family. This approach can further disadvantage marginalized family members by neglecting the fact that when they are viewed as sick or inadequate they can internalize these negative attitudes to such a degree that it prevents them from following their unique paths and attaining success.

THE *DR. PHIL* SHOW

An episode of the *Dr. Phil* show provided a good example of how mainstream psychology ignores the insights offered by the dynamics of family diversity and thus unwittingly contributes to the marginalization of nondominant subgroups.[1] The show focused on a mother and her five adult sons. The mother and four of her sons described themselves as responsible, hard working, and willing to make sacrifices for their financial security and success. The fifth son, Michael, referred to by Dr. Phil as the "black sheep," had run away from home as a teenager and been homeless most of the time over the next ten years, working at a paying job for only a few weeks now and then. He wore his hair longer than his brothers, had no health insurance, had sometimes asked his family for financial help, and dreamed of being a writer and artist. The mother and her four other sons not only disagreed with Michael's priorities and lifestyle, they felt he needed to change his errant ways and conform more to their expectations. The mother wanted Michael, like her other sons, to live a "clean and successful" life, and she desired a "close family," a wish thwarted by Michael's estrangement.

Consistent with mainstream psychology's usual approach to diversity, the family members did not see the family as consisting of diverse subgroups and treated Michael as if he alone had problems and had caused the family distress. However, the difficulties of this family can be better understood by looking at the family's diversity and how its dynamics marginalized Michael and gave power to the other family members as the dominant subgroup. From this perspective we can see that Michael's differences were not just a result of wayward beliefs or irresponsible behavior but that Michael was fundamentally a different kind of person. This is revealed when the mother and one brother recognized that Michael's divergence from the family norm had appeared way before issues of his irresponsibility and lifestyle ever arose. The mother said it was as if Michael had been dropped from an "alien spaceship," and one of the brothers said that Michael "was always so different." These statements suggest that Michael was inherently very different from the other members of his family.

Exploring this further, it seems evident that Michael had different values, perspectives, and communication styles from the rest of the family. Michael valued freedom and creativity, stressing that he didn't want a conventional nine-to-five job but instead hoped to be a writer and artist, and had already produced some exquisite paintings. By contrast, the rest of the family valued working hard to make money, believing that artistic interests should be pursued on weekends, or sacrificed if need be, to attain financial security. And while Michael was willing to leave home early and live an alternative lifestyle to pursue his dream of being an artist, the rest of the family valued the closeness achieved through their homogeneity. With regard to their differing communication styles, Michael was always kind in expressing his views about his lifestyle to the family; he listened to Dr. Phil and his own family members carefully and thoughtfully, never interrupting or being defensive. The mother and her four other sons, on the other hand, spoke authoritatively and critically about Michael, readily dismissing his point of view, putting him down, or interrupting him, showing no concern for the pain they were causing him. They spoke as if their way was the only way, insisting that they were all doing the "right thing."

Michael's differing values, perspectives, and communication styles, in conjunction with the hostility the mother and her four other sons directed at him, marginalized him as a subgroup. And like other marginalized subgroups of society, Michael was pathologized—viewed as sick, or deficient and in need of change. Rather than developing a tolerance or respect for his differences, they saw him as having an illness that Dr. Phil could help cure—and in fact stated their belief that Michael, and not any of them, needed psychological help.

While the family complained of Michael's estrangement from them they attributed this problem to Michael's pathology, not to the obvious fact that Michael was treated differently from the rest of the family. For example, after the mother admitted that Michael was always "alien" to her and the rest of the family, she said she didn't understand why he wasn't closer to the family, seeing no causal relationship between her view of Michael as alien and his estrangement.

Michael was also the target of the rest of the family's projections, blinding them from seeing him objectively as a person with his own weaknesses and strengths. For example, the family saw his values and goals that were at odds with their values and goals as his weaknesses and their strengths. While some family members acknowledged that they had artistic interests, they believed that following that path would be irresponsible and unrealistic, instead taking pride in the fact that they, unlike Michael, worked at jobs they didn't like to become more financially secure and successful. Projecting their values onto Michael's choices, they had become blind to the positive qualities reflected in Michael's pursuit of his dream, such as overcoming obstacles to living the life of an artist—the same obstacles that had stopped them from further pursuing their own artistic interests.

The mother's projection onto Michael can also been seen in her suggestion that his lifestyle was "unclean," a term almost always projected onto marginalized subgroups, suggesting their moral inferiority and justifying their lack of entitlement to social privilege. This kind of projection is often made in families that have "dirty laundry" hidden in their closet. For example, sometimes family members who have experienced the pain and shame of financial distress as the result of someone's risky decision go on to develop rigid attitudes toward family members who take risks. Or sometimes families that have lost a member to a "forbidden" life, causing trauma to those left behind, project their unprocessed resentment onto their children, grandchildren, and even people outside the family, seeing them as irresponsible, selfish, or heartless. And even though their ramifications ripple out like waves into future generations, such situations often remain undisclosed.

In addition to being pathologized and the target of others' projections, Michael, as a marginalized subgroup, was devalued. Implicit in the family's devaluation of him was a sense of superiority fueled by the belief that if everyone could be like them the world would be a better place—an attitude fundamental to discrimination. From their point of view, their focus on hard work, financial security, and family closeness made them valuable members of society. On the other hand, Michael's independence, his art, and his plans to write a children's book were not considered worthy endeavors. They believed that Michael had much to learn from them and would be a better person if he could make the kinds of sacrifices they made; however, they couldn't see how they might become better people by learning to make some financial sacrifices to pursue their creative lives or become more independent like Michael.

Dr. Phil's responses to these issues showed the limitations of the mainstream approach to family diversity. Rather than looking at the family in terms of its diversity, Dr. Phil sided with its dominant subgroup in marginalizing Michael. He didn't seem to notice that the family projected their own views onto Michael, saw him as deficient and in need of change, and devalued him; instead, he supported the family's dominant subgroup in a unified effort to change Michael into what the family believed to be a "responsible" adult on a successful life path. He diagnosed Michael as irresponsible, undisciplined, and unrealistic, as if these qualities alone formed the root of the family's difficulties, without addressing the rest of the family's shortcomings—their critical demeanor, ignorance, rigidity, and prejudice. For example, he confronted Michael about how infrequently he had worked at a real "money-making" job, how he didn't have health insurance, and how little progress he had made with his writing project. He repeatedly showed Michael how his irresponsibility and lack of work ethic had led to his financial circumstances and lack of progress in his chosen field. For instance, when Michael said that he hadn't asked his family for money, Dr. Phil pointed out how he had, in fact, relied on their help when he had become sick. Accepting the family's perspective, Dr. Phil focused on aligning Michael's values with the values of the family, believing that being more disciplined and realistic would even help Michael achieve his own goals of being a writer and artist. Further, Dr. Phil failed to challenge the family's projections onto Michael, allowing them to see Michael in terms of qualities they viewed as negative. He never considered how Michael could be an inspiration for the other family members to pursue their own artistic interests or how their sacrifices for financial security and family closeness had prevented them from being happier or more fulfilled. In addition, he never considered delving into the family history to investigate the root of the family's focus on financial security and success.

ALTERNATE PSYCHOLOGICAL APPROACHES TO FAMILY DIVERSITY

Several alternate psychological approaches consider the dynamics of family diversity in ways that benefit all members of the family. One such approach is Structural Family Therapy, a family systems theory developed by Salvador Minuchin. According to this approach, family members forming coalitions against another member is a sign of dysfunction. Minuchin observed that such families, like the one on the *Dr. Phil* show, often view one member in need of help and send that family member to individual therapy. Minuchin called that person the "identified patient."[2] To Minuchin, the identified patient is not the problem but is simply used as a scapegoat for the rest of the family to avoid delving deeper into the root causes of their problems. In fact, for a family systems therapist to help one member of the family the whole family must be helped, a perspective that prevents a family from devaluing and marginalizing the identified patient.

Another approach that considers the dynamics of family diversity in ways that help all members is process-oriented psychology. Arnold Mindell, Ph.D., the founder of process-oriented psychology, has shown that the identified patient is actually expressing feelings, thoughts, beliefs, or behaviors that other family members have disavowed, and that understanding these expressions is integral to the family's health and wholeness. Thus, the identified patient serves as a useful projection screen for the qualities the rest of the family does not want to accept or integrate. Further, Mindell has demonstrated that when family members recognize these repudiated aspects of themselves and integrate them, family conflicts are resolved, they operate better as a team, and the identified patient is no longer devalued and marginalized. In reality, the identified patient becomes an essential part of the cure.

I witnessed a powerful demonstration of this phenomenon at a workshop facilitated by Mindell in the mid-1990s, where over a hundred people gathered on the Oregon coast to study the psychology of physical symptoms. One participant suffered from Tourette's syndrome, a neurological disorder characterized by repetitive, involuntary movements and vocalizations, especially the use of obscene language. In the midst of thoughtful discussions, he would shout out words such as *shit, crap,* and *dammit,* despite making an effort to prevent such outbursts. After each one, we all went on as if nothing had occurred, assuming they had nothing to do with our workshop until, after one outburst, Mindell asked the man what would happen if he didn't hold back at all. The man immediately began to uninhibitedly rant and curse. Mindell then asked the rest of us to make our own sounds. A sound of great joy arose as we all yelled out such phrases as "I don't agree!" "Shut up!" "I need a break!" "What about my problems?" "Let's get on with it!" The man with Tourette's syndrome roared with laughter and happiness. We had joined *his* culture; we had stopped seeing him as the sick person who needed to be cured and had integrated his disturbing qualities by interrupting with disagreements and vulgar language. After this initial experiment, Mindell proposed that over the next few days we all speak up more, interrupt spontaneously if we were not satisfied, and generally be less polite and more demanding about what we wanted from the seminar. Much to the group's amazement, not only did the seminar become more lively but the man with Tourette's syndrome hardly made a peep. Some might think we had a healing effect on him; however, I like to think that he healed us—the culture of obedient students who listened to their teacher without interruption, demands, or expressions of dissatisfaction. Mindell would argue that we healed each other and made the group more whole.

Applying this approach to Michael and his family on the *Dr. Phil* show would lead us to challenge the family's assumption that they were there to heal Michael and consider ways in which Michael represented a potential for healing them. Dr. Phil correctly challenged Michael to become more like the rest of the family, suggesting that a bit more ambition and responsibility could also help Michael advance his career as a writer and artist. However, it also seemed apparent that the rest of the family could have benefited from Michael's independence, willingness to make sacrifices for his creative life, and ability to communicate with more openness and caring.

I witnessed another interesting example of identified patient as healer while teaching a critical thinking class. In this class, a discussion focused on a student, who, as the mother of four children, had risen through corporate ranks by being extremely exacting and reliable. A straight A student, she was always present and participating, never having missed a class in two years, even when she had a fever. She told us that two of her daughters had made it to the state softball finals, but the game was out of town and the only way for her to take them would be to either miss class or drive all night after class to arrive by morning. Some students in this predicament would have just taken the night off and not worried about missing class, especially if their grades were good, but not this woman.

As the class discussion deepened, I learned that one of her children "really struggled," as she put it, while the others were "doing well." The struggling child did not like school, wanted to be an artist but, like Michael, hadn't produced much art, and had had several run-ins with the police as a result of marijuana use. He was a "dreamer who wanted to help the world," she said dismissively. From her perspective, he was undisciplined, irresponsible, and not committed. He was an outsider in the family, a marginalized subgroup, the identified patient.

However, it soon became apparent that this woman projected the qualities of irresponsibility and lack of discipline and commitment onto her son. When I asked her what she would do if she had no responsibilities or worries, she said, eyes moistening, she would open a shelter for injured animals as a way of contributing to a better world. While this dream deeply moved her, she believed that pursuing it would be irresponsible. It became evident that her son, whom she had dismissed as a dreamer, represented her disavowed qualities, which were nonetheless a very important part of her. Even though she said she wasn't willing to leave her job to open the animal shelter, she nevertheless needed the qualities inherent in that dream—the ability to nurture and the desire to help create a better world—to face other challenges in her life, such as understanding and connecting with her son and missing a class for her two daughters.

Taking the dynamics of family diversity into consideration, I suggested that she talk to her son about her dream of establishing an animal shelter. Two weeks later, she reported that he had really opened up to her and they felt close for the first time in a long while. She had come to appreciate that her son, despite criticism and pressure, had the strength to hold on to his dream; that he, too, was exacting and reliable, only about different things; and that they were more like each other than either had thought. Not only did he have something to learn from her, but she had found she could be a lot more like him, and this new attitude had fostered a better relationship between them.

Michael's family would also likely enjoy a new kind of relationship built on mutual respect and understanding if all members made an effort to change their perspective. For example, instead of marginalizing and devaluing Michael, the mother and her four sons might follow Michael's lead and consider how they have sacrificed some of their own dreams for material and egoistic ends. They could also benefit from adopting the kindness and openness Michael had shown in communication.

But according to family systems theory, for family members to change they would need to gain increased awareness of their strengths, weaknesses, and how they could learn from each other to become more whole. Thus, Michael would need to see how he could benefit from embracing some of the family's qualities; and the rest of the family would need to see how they might benefit from adopting some of his qualities.

Process-oriented psychology adds a new perspective to the problem of marginalized family members internalizing the negative attitudes of disapproving family members to the extent it keeps them from pursuing their own goals by assuming the marginalized individuals are not in need of fixing but rather require support to follow their own paths. Many family members who have been marginalized by their families, including numerous gays and lesbians, internalize the dominant family members' values to such a degree that they spend years, if not their whole lives, fighting those values but never having the support or inner strength to abandon them and follow their own paths. As long as this happens, their families continue to devalue and marginalize them, working to convert or enlighten them about the error of their ways. But once they make a more complete break from the dominant members' values and begin to be true to themselves, either they develop a new closeness to the family or they achieve a cleaner separation so they can follow their own life path without criticism.

For example, I once worked with a woman whose family, like Michael's, valued financial security and family homogeneity. As a child, she had been an excellent student and appeared to be aiming at the same goals as her sister and parents. While she had always adored the arts, she went to work for an insurance company, earning a good wage and acquiring numerous benefits. But she became increasingly unhappy with her job and after three years decided to leave and pursue an artist's life, accepting a part-time job with considerably less income and no benefits. For a while she lived between two worlds, fully dedicated to neither her creative dreams nor her financial security and success. One day when I asked her what the biggest difference was between her and the rest of her family, she promptly said, "None of them is happy." Growing up she heard her father preach about the need to make sacrifices, but he was always moody. She saw her mother make sacrifices but never speak up for herself, thinking she had to put up with poor treatment to maintain her job and keep her relationship with her husband free of conflict. And she saw her sister, who likewise loved the arts, pursue an MBA because it would lead to a higher-paying job. In contrast to the rest of her family, she wanted to be creative and happy. However, not until she could fully accept her own calling as an artist was she able to let go of the values the rest of her family shared and dedicate herself to pursuing an artist's life.

Similarly, if Michael were able to follow his dream of becoming a writer and artist with increased dedication and not internalize his family's devaluation of his attributes and goals, they would likely give up trying to change him, at which point the energy he expends on countering his family's criticisms could be used to make his own dream come true. His family members may even become closer again, based not on their sameness but on respect for their differences and a new awareness that they can learn from each another. Consequently, supporting Michael to live closer to his values and dreams, rather than trying to correct and chastise him, might be a wiser intervention.

CONCLUSION

Diversity in society entails a variety of subgroups with different ranks and privileges, some of which are devalued and marginalized. While the same is true for families, practitioners of mainstream psychology typically do not take the dynamics of diversity into account when working with families. Instead, they often adopt the dominant family members' point of view and thus treat marginalized family members as if they are sick or inadequate and in need of help rather than facilitating learning and growth within the family system by treating the whole family as the patient and showing members how they can come to respect and learn from each other.

This is how Dr. Phil responded to the family on his show, aligning himself with the mother and her four other sons and treating Michael as if he needed to learn from his family while they had nothing to learn from him. Such a perspective further devalues the family member already marginalized. By contrast, the approaches of family systems therapy and process-oriented psychology, rather than focusing only on marginalized members, consider the dynamics of family diversity, resulting in enhanced healing for the whole family.

Marginalized family members endure the same pain and suffering, as well as the poverty, violence, depression, and substance abuse as marginalized subgroups of society. But instead of people seeing the diversity they represent as a rich source of experience and wisdom, they are often viewed as inadequate or even threatening, and coerced into conforming to the values of the dominant family members.

Looking at this dynamic from a wider perspective, in a sense all communities, societies, and nations comprise one big family. Some people are better aligned with dominant cultures, while others are more marginalized and seen as outsiders because of their lifestyle, age, health, appearance, preferences, beliefs, feelings, or behaviors. But the truth is no marginalized person is the patient or the problem and no one belonging to a dominant subgroup is the teacher. We each have lessons to learn and to teach, and healing is something we all do together.

Passion through the Ages

Sex and Shame

*Perhaps no aspect of human activity has been as
dysfunctionally shamed as our sexuality.*
—John Bradshaw

SEXUALITY HAS BEEN USED TO SHAME PEOPLE for centuries, inhibiting sexual expression, confusing individuals about their natural impulses, and marginalizing groups whose sexual practices deviate from societal norms. The fact that we often come to learn about sexuality in conflicted ways contributes to our confusion about it and makes us vulnerable to being shamed about our sexuality. As youths, we have sexual desires we are often told to suppress, which communicates the message that something is wrong with our sexual impulses. Or we are given no message at all and are thus left to negotiate hormones, desires, the need for safety, and nuances of intimacy on our own. Amplifying the difficulty are the many confusing and hurtful messages about sexuality that we encounter daily in society, such as young girls being sexualized, women being objectified, and boys and men portrayed as predatory.

Consequently, it is not surprising that people feel vulnerable discussing sexuality or that approaches to sex education or counseling about sexuality are sometimes hotly debated. For example, when the topic of sexuality comes up in my college classes students first respond with giggles and jokes, often followed by heated arguments focusing on moral and political views about abortion, gay marriage, and parenting. Other students refuse to discuss the issues at all, citing their belief that debating these viewpoints in class is inappropriate. In human services or counseling classes, the conversation becomes more personal as students share their experiences working with children or adults who have been sexually abused. But only rarely, whether in the classroom or outside among friends or colleagues, do people talk about their own experiences of sexuality.

Most of us erect boundaries when it comes to talking about sexuality to protect the sanctity of our sexual feelings and desires from the violation of being shamed. Because of the powerful need for protection when it comes to issues of sexuality, many people look to psychological counsel, in the form of books, therapists, or programs for guidance. Some forms of guidance help people in a nonjudgmental way to know their needs, interests, sensitivities, and histories. But when mainstream psychology looks to deviations from social norms as a measure of sexual health or appropriateness it shames people. Most often, mainstream psychological approaches have a moralistic orientation, directing people to look at themselves as if there is something ethically or psychologically wrong with them if their behavior deviates from social norms. This type of counsel can turn people against themselves and the culture against certain forms of sexual expression, resulting in the marginalization of particular groups, as it did with regard to homosexuals in the twentieth century and still today.

THE *DR. PHIL* SHOW

An episode of the *Dr. Phil* show provided a good example of how mainstream psychology uses moralistic principles and cultural stereotypes to counsel a person about their sexuality.[1] The show had two guests: a woman in her fifties, who had been married for many years until her husband passed away, and her son, who was in his mid-twenties. The woman had dated several men in their twenties; her son objected to her behavior, saying that she danced with his friends, wore sexually provocative clothing in his presence, and should instead "act her age." He said it was more appropriate for her to be sitting on the couch reading a book.

Dr. Phil challenged the woman's pattern of relationships, implying that her sexual interest in younger men was inappropriate. Responding with belittling humor, statements masquerading as questions, and comparisons that played on inaccurate caricatures and personal biases, he suggested that she was too promiscuous, "hopping around" from bed to bed. He compared her behavior to that of older men dating younger women, saying, sarcastically, that her behavior made him think of fathers dating their daughters. He then reinforced this message by evoking the image of a bald fat man and a sexy long-legged woman to further convey his meaning, implying that the woman's behavior was not only ridiculous but lewd, and even abusive. In comparing her behavior to that of men who were disgusting or incestuous, he provoked feelings of outrage associated with incest and sexual abuse. While some people might consider Dr. Phil's responses harmless humor, his remarks were actually thinly veiled judgments of the woman as measured against acceptable and unacceptable standards for middle-aged women. Framing her behavior in this way closed the door to any deeper discussion of her needs and desires and taught the audience that behavior such as hers calls for moral education rather than psychological exploration.

Uncomfortable with his innuendos, the woman asked Dr. Phil to be more direct and simply say if he thought what she was doing was wrong. Instead of taking this opportunity to directly express his opinion, however, he avoided the issue, saying she looked "goofy." If he had instead stated that he felt her behavior reflected a form of sexual deviance or was too offensive to her son's sensibilities, as his allusions and comparisons had implied, the woman would have had a chance to agree or disagree; but disguising his accusations in provocative images made the public shaming of the woman less obvious and difficult to challenge.

Dr. Phil continued to shame the woman when considering the thoughts and feelings of her son. He empathized with the son's sensibilities, likening his distress to that of a twenty-five-year-old man he knew who had objected to seeing his mother and father snuggling on the couch, believing that, in both these cases, the parents were putting their children in stressful situations. Dr. Phil never emphasized that the sons were not children and never questioned their attitudes toward their mothers, even though their views were worthy of critical reflection. In fact, Dr. Phil's perspective was so extreme as to imply that children, regardless of their age, should not witness their parents engaging in the even the mildest forms of sexual expression, such as snuggling—thus regarding their parents as virtually sexless. These messages served as a lesson not only to the woman on the show but to all members of the audience who had ever been so shamed about their sexuality that they were likely to accept Dr. Phil's unquestioned authority on this issue.

Dr. Phil's response to the woman ignored the merit of exploring society's stereotypes concerning middle-aged women's sexuality. In addition, his approach failed to teach her or his audience to investigate their sexuality in a way that fosters self-trust, critical thinking, and a deepened understanding of their needs and desires. Instead, it taught them that there are rules to follow and deviations from these rules are unnatural and immoral. Consequently, Dr. Phil became a judge instead of a counselor, and the audience became a condemning jury rather than open-minded learners.

THE DESTRUCTIVE MESSAGES OF SHAME

Shame is called the master emotion because it affects our most fundamental experience of ourselves and the way we evaluate and understand all other experiences. It puts a filtering lens between us and the world, causing us to interpret others and evaluate ourselves in terms of deficiencies.

Shame delivers at least three destructive messages. First, it teaches people to distrust or dismiss their feelings. This is disastrous when it comes to sexuality, an issue in which feelings are essential to making critical distinctions between being loved and being hurt, being courageous and taking inappropriate risks, or asserting ourselves and being insensitive. In addition, understanding and trusting our feelings is a prerequisite to being honest, loving, and intimate with others. No intellectual understanding can aid us in sharing true intimacy like our own trusted feelings.

Second, shame teaches people not to challenge authorities or think critically about sexuality, leaving all decision-making power over what is right and wrong in the hands of others. It consequently teaches us that we alone are the cause of our suffering and that blaming others is the result of our erroneous perceptions. This dynamic is most destructive in cases of sexual abuse, where victims are coached by authority figures to believe that they are the cause of their own victimization. Where sexual abusers are invested in protecting themselves from blame and strong ideologies abound (including those regarding race, gender, and sexual preference), it is particularly important that all discussions about sexuality and sex education encourage learners to use their capacity for critical thinking and to challenge authorities.

Finally, shame teaches people not to investigate the needs and desires underlying their sexual impulses because they arise from a "flawed nature." When needs and desires are treated as pathologies that require fixing, they are replaced with rules for how to behave. This is why it is important that all discussions of sexuality and sex education seek to reveal the deeper needs and desires that underlie sexual impulses.

In my experience with groups of students and clients, lurking behind painful jokes, innuendos, condemnations, and other strategies that shame sexuality are often unprocessed traumas or unexamined needs and desires. While such shaming strategies may give people the momentary illusion of being protected from facing trauma or exploring deep needs and desires, the cost is great. These strategies undermine people's trust in their own feelings and thus their capacity for self-respect, establishing proper boundaries, and differentiating love from harm. They also subject people to the unquestioned authority of others, keep people looking for fixes to their faulty natures, suppress diversity, and marginalize groups—such as, in the case of the *Dr. Phil* show, middle-aged women who express themselves sexually with younger men.

ALTERNATIVE APPROACH TO COUNSELING PEOPLE ABOUT SEXUALITY

In contrast to many mainstream psychological approaches to counseling people about their sexuality, or sex education, a love-based approach offers a way to understand and support people's sexuality without shaming them. For the woman on the *Dr. Phil* show, a love-based approach would first take into account cultural norms, stereotypes, and biases that may be influencing her thoughts and behaviors. For example, a love-based approach would consider cultural messages sent to middle-aged women about their sexuality, including the notion that they have little sexual drive; that beauty, health, strength, and virility are associated with youth; and that while middle-aged men in our culture are still seen as virile and sexual, middle-aged women are not. Assuming she has internalized one or more of these messages, it would focus on freeing her from its constraints, allowing her to express her sexuality more congruently, and educating the people around her about the hurtfulness of the offending message.

Next a love-based approach would explore the woman's deeper needs and desires, assuming that her attraction to younger men is an important indication of them. Doing so would eliminate the atmosphere of shame insinuating that her interest is nothing more than a form of deviance. It would also take into account the fact that many women who have become wives and mothers when young, cutting short the exploration of themselves sexually, are often not supported when they later resume their sexual development.

A love-based approach would also determine what had attracted the woman to young men, perhaps discovering that it was their beauty, energy, openness, and aliveness—qualities that she might want to be more in touch with in herself, despite their cultural association with youth. That is, she might not want to fit the stereotype of a woman her age, and hence this might not be the time for her to live within the confines of her twenty-five-year-old son's expectations. This behavior would be more in line with Alfred Kinsey's groundbreaking research on male and female sexuality, in which he astonished the mainstream public by speaking of the marginal differences between men and women's sexual desires in contrast to prior beliefs that women were less sexual then men.[2] Before Kinsey, and still to some extent today, women who experienced a strong sex drive were judged as dirty, ungodly, or pathological, and their interest in sexual activity was often shamed.

If Dr. Phil had expressed the viewpoint that there was no reason for a woman in her fifties, with no spouse and only adult children, to live as if she were over the hill, that it was time for her son to consider his mother a woman and not just his mother, and that she shouldn't be confined by the cultural stereotypes about middle-aged women, no doubt many women in the audience would have empathized with her and supported her fight against a culture that desexualizes women her age rather than align themselves with Dr. Phil and the culture's stereotypes. In short, taking this woman's behavior as worthy of further exploration would likely reveal needs and desires that lead to understanding rather than shaming.

Finally, a love-based approach would take a person's resistance to following the advice of any counselor, book, or program as an assertion of their authority and worthy of support, and consequently view the woman's challenge to Dr. Phil's message as important and advise him to be more direct with his opinions. This would affirm the woman's feelings, awareness, and empowerment, giving her support as she explored her sexuality. Thus a love-based approach would aid the woman in building a trusting relationship with her feelings; support her resistance to authority; further the exploration of her needs and desires; counter shaming that could inhibit her in the future; and help her gain freedom from stereotypes and biases that might limit her happiness.

EXPLORING SEXUALITY WITHOUT SHAME

We need approaches to counseling people that do not shame their sexuality and that help them trust their feelings, investigate their deeper needs and desires, and support their critical thinking. The following exercises can be used to help explore sexuality in beneficial ways without shame.

Building a Bridge of Trust to Feelings

The sex education available from parents, religious institutions, community, and the media not only delivers mixed messages but often appeals only to our minds and not our emotions, suggesting that our feelings and bodies can't be trusted. However, the confusion and pain many people suffer in relationship to sexuality derives largely from difficulty with feelings.

Fear, desire, insecurity, vulnerability, tenderness, care, love, guilt, shame, pain, and trauma invariably need to be a part of any deep conversation about sexuality.

Exploring our feelings requires a shame-free zone where we don't evaluate them but instead listen to their messages. The following exercise helps build a bridge of trust to feelings.

a. Think about a sexual moment you had, and ask yourself which feelings you thought were wrong and should be dismissed or not communicated.

b. Ask yourself what your feelings would say if they could speak.

c. Determine what keeps you from communicating these feelings about the sexual moment to your partner, counselor, or other individuals with whom you share your views. Pay particular attention to feelings associated with proceeding slowly, hesitating, or being insecure, as well as feelings associated with proceeding quickly, excitedly, and confidently. These are the feelings that connect us with the "yes" and "no" of going forward with a sexual moment.

Learning to Think Critically and Challenge Authorities

When sexuality is approached without dialogue and when sex education is one-sided, judgmental, and moralistic, people are not protected from the shame that often accompanies sexual exploration or the stereotypes and biases asserted by a culture. Although educators may have strong moral views about what is appropriate or inappropriate with regard to sexuality, a shame-free sexual education requires clearly stating those values, allowing others to challenge the advice proffered by such authorities, and supporting critical thinking about the issue. The following exercise helps support critical thinking and the capacity to challenge authorities.

a. Ask yourself what judgments others might have of your sexuality.

b. Ask yourself how you would challenge these people.

c. Ask yourself what would keep you from challenging these people.

d. Ask yourself what judgments you have about other people's sexuality.

e. Ask yourself how these people might challenge you concerning your judgments about them.

Investigating Deeper Needs and Desires

Often our initial impulses, including sexual impulses, are just the tip of the iceberg. Dr. Arnold Mindell calls these initial impulses that catch our attention "flirts."[3] Why they catch our attention is rarely obvious at first; to make that determination we need to explore them further.

For example, I never loved the taste of blue cheese but nonetheless had a desire to sample more types of it. Blue cheese flirted with me and led me to better understand what I desired in my life. To learn more about why I was drawn to blue cheese, I tasted it very slowly and experienced an explosion of pungent and forceful flavor. In this way, I realized it was not so much the blue cheese that I desired but its powerful direct contact and wanted more of that in my life—not just with food but also with people and ideas.

Sexuality is full of flirts, which can be in such forms as textures, shapes, colors, images, feelings, and fantasies. Finding out what is at the root of these flirts requires exploration, which can be done in the following ways.

a. Ask yourself what impulses, fantasies, or sexual activities attract you. Focusing on such things as images, tactual sensations, smells, tastes, and sounds, describe them in detail.

b. Write a short poem to these experiences. Then read the poem out loud, perhaps to a lover, and talk about how its themes and imagery are important in different areas of your life.

Exploring sexuality in these ways can increase self-knowledge, help liberate us from shame and cultural bias, and assist us in understanding our deeper needs and desires.

CONCLUSION

The fact that we learn about our sexuality in conflicted ways and encounter confusing and frequently hurtful messages about it impedes our ability to trust our feelings, challenge authority, and explore our needs and desires. Young girls are often sexualized, and women are regularly objectified. Boys and men are repeatedly portrayed as predatory and treated as if "getting hard" is a sign of sexual health, as if sex requires no intimacy. Older men who express their sexuality are often seen as dirty, and older women who explore their sexuality as lewd. These sexual judgments and stereotypes not only cause harm but give license for people to shame those whose expressions of sexuality may deviate from the norm.

Because our sexuality is so often shamed, we must give careful consideration to the counsel we offer others about their sexuality. To protect our children, students, or anyone who comes to us for counsel from shame's destructive effects, we must help them build a bridge to their feelings, support their critical thinking and challenging of authority, and be open to understanding their needs and desires.

Breaking It Down

Black Youths, Sports, and Education

> *It is their faith in the game that unites their family and*
> *gives each person hope. And it is this faith that ultimately allows them*
> *to build upon their failures as well as their triumphs and make for*
> *themselves a potentially better life.*
> —Roger Ebert, discussing the movie *Hoop Dreams*

PRACTITIONERS OF MAINSTREAM PSYCHOLOGY tend to treat the problems and aspirations of black youths and middle-class white youths similarly, disregarding the substantial differences that exist between them due to social history and thus not adequately educating the public about these differences. Such lack of perspective is especially evident with regard to mainstream psychology's view of the predisposition of some black youths to focus on achievements in sports to the exclusion of success in academics. To understand how this predisposition of black youths differs from that of white youths, it is necessary to look at some significant aspects of the history of race and sports in America.

The complex history of race and sports in America is, in part, a story of the struggle by blacks to refute the belief that they are inferior, not only intellectually and spiritually but also physically. In the early twentieth century, some important events in this struggle took place in the boxing ring. At that time in America, black boxers could fight professionally, even against whites, but the heavyweight championship was considered a competition for whites only, as the possibility of a black man winning the title was too incendiary an idea.[1] Nevertheless, the formidable black boxer Jack Johnson relentlessly pursued opportunities to fight for the title, finally winning both battles in 1908 after fighting and defeating the white boxer Tommy Burns. This victory by a black boxer caused an uproar among whites, who saw it as a humiliation to their race. The well-respected novelist Jack London then called for a "great white hope" to recapture the title and assert white superiority.[2] Jim Jeffries, who had held the title before retiring to avoid fighting Johnson, represented that hope. Jeffries said, "I feel obligated to the sporting public at least to make an effort to reclaim the heavyweight championship for the white race."[3] However, his effort was unsuccessful; in 1910, Johnson defeated him and held on to the title, a victory that prompted joyful celebration by blacks and rioting by whites.

Other milestones of black pride, achievement, and celebration in sports came in 1947 when Jackie Robinson signed a contract with the Brooklyn Dodgers and became the first black baseball player in modern times to play major league baseball and when Muhammad Ali stood as a black champion against the Vietnam War. Even today there is a special feeling of racial pride associated with the successes of champion golfer Tiger Woods, winning tennis players Venus and Serena Williams, and black coaches Tony Dungy and Lovie Smith, whose teams faced each other in the 2007 Super Bowl.

It is historical moments like these that provide the social context for some black youths to focus on excellence in sports even if it means having less success in academics. Black achievement in sports has ultimately carved out a path to respect for blacks, overcoming injustice and even racism whenever blacks and whites have competed together without discrimination—a worthy tradition to pass on to black youths of today.

However, while there has been movement toward recognition, respect, and equality in sports, biases and stereotypes still exist. For example, there is a persistent notion that black athletic ability goes hand in hand with lack of intellectual capacity; coaching and executive positions in sports should be held by whites; and the role of quarterback is best filled by white men. Also, corporations and the media have exploited the idea that blacks have natural physical ability rather than natural intellect to bring them rewards, as suggested by certain ads for sneakers. In short, while there is some wind at the back of black youths who dream of achievement in sports there is a wind at the front of black youths who desire achievement in academics.

THE *DR. PHIL* SHOW

An episode of the *Dr. Phil* show about the predisposition of black youths to focus on sports to the exclusion of academics provided insights into how ignoring the historical context of such a problem can create false impressions about black youths.[4] Dr. Phil's presentation began with an introduction by Samuel L. Jackson, who had played the lead role in the movie *Coach Carter*, a film about a real-life black basketball coach whose fierce determination and discipline on and off the court propelled several inner-city black youths to succeed in both athletics and academics beyond all expectations. Coach Carter, in fighting against the forces that prevented many black youths from achieving excellence in both academics and sports, became a hero. The movie's message is that inner-city black youths need more than dreams of achievement in sports; they also need hard-nosed and courageous elders who will hold their feet to the fire to keep the youths committed to excelling in academics even if their families, schools, and communities do not. The movie provided the context of the show, which featured two black youths focusing on becoming professional athletes at the expense of their academic studies, accompanied by their mothers, Jackson, Coach Carter, and Coach Carter's son.

In the ensuing discussion about the black youths' priorities, Dr. Phil declared that their dreams of being professional athletes "got in the way of reality," a message reinforced by Jackson, Coach Carter, and Coach Carter's son. Dr. Phil then challenged their viewpoint in an effort to hold them accountable for their poor efforts and grades in academic subjects. For example, he noted that the report card of one youth contained Fs in all subjects other than physical education, saying that his focus on athletics was an excuse to not study. And when the other youth said that his focus "gets lost," Dr. Phil emphasized his inconsistency, pointing out that his focus was fine on the ball field.

Dr. Phil then challenged the youths' mothers, implying that their disregard for enforcing discipline with respect to the youths' education was contributing to their sons' low grades, poor efforts, and bad attitudes about their futures. Echoing the message of the movie, Dr. Phil told them that more discipline and focus on academics was necessary if they expected their sons to have any opportunity to succeed in life.

On this episode of the *Dr. Phil* show, race was the "elephant in the room," implicitly part of the show's broader context, although there was never any discussion of how issues of race in America had contributed to the youths' priorities and predicament. In contrast to a typical episode of the *Dr. Phil* show, terms like "inner city," the presence of four powerful black men, and concerns raised by a movie about the problems of black youth all gave the impression that this was in many ways a black story. But while Dr. Phil deserves praise for inviting black elders to serve as experts, adding credibility and power to his message, he failed to highlight how systemic variables had undoubtedly influenced his guests. For example, while Dr. Phil noted that the movie *Coach Carter* was based on a true story that took place in Richmond, California, where boys are 80 percent more likely to go to prison than college, he used this statistic to emphasize the need for discipline with respect to encouraging academic achievement rather than discussing social factors that create racial inequity in educational and criminal justice systems.

Dr. Phil said that the youths' dreams of becoming professional athletes "get in the way of reality" since not many people are able to achieve this goal. However, he failed to say that five of the six young men profiled in *Coach Carter* who did go to college went on athletic scholarships. He also did not mention that for blacks achievement in sports is a source of pride and means of competing on a level playing field, which is often not the case in academics. And when Dr. Phil urged one of the women, a single mother, to provide more discipline, he did not acknowledge the parenting difficulties black single mothers encounter due to getting lower wages, having problems accessing child care, and facing greater risks raising children in the inner city. In addition, he neglected to speak about the psychic pain associated with the dominant culture's stereotypes involving black single mothers, an impact that was evident when the mother said to Dr. Phil, "I'm always the bad one." Further, while Dr. Phil's position of privilege—as a white male who is rich, famous, and respected as a national authority—does not discredit his ability to advise a single black mother, these differences should have been acknowledged, especially since the advice was given in a public forum to educate millions of viewers.

Leaving the "elephant" of race unacknowledged made direct discussion about its effects on the issues raised impossible and allowed the audience to revert to stereotypical thoughts about and projections on black youths— that they lack intelligence and tend to revolt against the system—and single black mothers—that they have children without taking responsibility for raising them. Without some historical and sociological perspective about race and sports in America, it was too easy to conclude that the black youths' dream of achievement in sports occurred because they were delinquent and naive; that black mothers lack the discipline to ensure their sons' academic success; and that white middle-class audience members are outsiders looking in at a black problem that has nothing to do with them or the culture at large. While hard work and individual responsibility are important ingredients in any success equation, they do not constitute the entire formula. When this kind of incomplete description of a problem is sent out over the airwaves, it can easily reinforce stereotypes rather than open minds and hearts to more complex individual, family, social, and political dilemmas that face our nation.

TOWARD A MORE COMPLETE ANALYSIS

A love-based alternative to mainstream psychology's understanding of the predicament black male youths face when they dream of achievement in sports at the expense of academic excellence, as expressed on the *Dr. Phil* show, would take into account historical, social, and cultural conditions that provide a context for the circumstances. First, any analysis of the dilemma would consider the quality of the education provided to black inner-city youths. Schools in poor inner-city neighborhoods usually lack resources, employ less skilled and experienced teachers (higher teacher turnover results from good teachers moving to better-funded schools), and have more crowded classrooms than schools in wealthy suburbs, which typically spend almost twice as much per student.[5] According to the US Department of Education, fourth-grade students in poor areas are three grades behind students in wealthier areas.[6] Moreover, the Harvard Civil Rights Project predicts that as courts withdraw their support for integrating schools and schools become more segregated, such discrepancies will only increase.[7]

In addition to these physical realties, the relatively fewer resources and lower quality of teaching sends a negative psychological message to students. Jonathan Kozol says, in *Savage Inequalities*, "Students are given a direct measure of their social worth and future chances by the amount of money they see being spent on their education."[8] Another factor that sends a message about social worth, according to the National Center of Education Statistics, is the quality of security. Black students are more likely to attend schools that have security guards, metal detectors, security cameras, and bars on windows[9]—all of which reinforce their psychic equivalents. In addition to these disadvantages, a Georgetown University study investigating whether earning a college degree was worth the investment found that black students who go on to get a college degree generally earn significantly less than whites earn in the same profession.[10] Certainly such conditions contribute to the 50 percent inner-city dropout rate and make the allure of achievement in sports greater and that of academic success less.[11] These conditions should lead us to point an accusatory finger not only at underachieving black youths and their mothers but also at schools, school systems, and a culture that is too often blind to the extent of their predicament.

Second, an alternative approach to analyzing the dilemma black youths face when they dream of achievement in sports at the expense of academics would consider how they are influenced by the stereotypes reinforced by society. To enhance business, American corporations build an image of the natural black athlete as having special physical ability. Nathan McCall, in his book *What's Going On: Personal Essays*, calls attention to ads such as Gatorade's "Be Like Mike," Reebok's "This Is *My* Planet," and Nike's "The Revolution Is about Basketball," all featuring several black NBA stars and aimed at their achievement in sports with the intention of evoking feelings of black pride and selling sneakers.[12]

Society's stereotypes and projections also play a role in perpetuating this image. While the belief that blacks are natural athletes may seem to imply appreciation and praise, it is almost always attached to two unspoken diminishing beliefs: first, if athletic capacity is natural then it is not really the result of hard work, dedication, and character; and second, if blacks are naturally gifted physically they must be relatively less gifted intellectually. The mainstream acceptance of black athletes and their celebrity status inadvertently feeds these less conscious stereotypes, making focus on achievement in athletics for black youths a double-edged sword. It means that pursuing a highly prized role in sports leads to being stereotyped and, perhaps worse, being vulnerable to the self-hatred that can result from closely identifying with, as author and professor Michael Eric Dyson puts it, "big, black, masculine, athleticized, and eroticized bodies" to the exclusion of other qualities, like intelligence and creativity.[13] This insidious form of self-hatred engenders a lack of self-confidence that makes endeavors requiring intelligence much harder to pursue. Stereotypes of the black athlete and black body that highlight physicality and minimize the intellect increase the difficulty of not only the path to academic success for blacks but also the fight against social ignorance. This makes Dr. Phil's message even more important and also increases the need for our collective understanding.

Finally, an alternative approach to any analysis of the dilemma black youths face when they dream of achievement in sports at the expense of academics would consider that a career in professional sports has a different meaning and context for blacks than whites because of its association with the struggle for racial and social equality. Today's acceptance of African Americans as professional athletes was earned on the backs of blacks who suffered in the past. Later successes became symbols of pride and steps to social equality that were not always lauded by the mainstream culture, such as when Hank Aaron closed in on Babe Ruth's records and was demonized. Thus for blacks, achievement in sports represents a path of pride as well as a trail away from prejudice. The history of race and sports should not be seen only in terms of physical ability; it should also be viewed in terms of the qualities of courage, perseverance, moral authority, pride, and yes, intelligence.

CONCLUSION

For black youths the path of achievement in sports holds many prizes, including pride, self-esteem, and potential celebrity status, while the path of achievement in academics is discouraged by the system and fraught with messages that demean and diminish. If psychology is to encourage black youths to achieve excellence in academics, especially in relation to their participation in sports, it must acknowledge the motivations blacks have to pursue sports—to feel beautiful, proud, courageous, and esteemed—in the context of historical, social, and cultural factors. To omit these aspects is to limit the scope of solutions by ignoring the deeper hopes and dreams of black youths and placing the weight of their academic disadvantage, much of which is societal not parental, on the shoulders of their mothers. In moving forward, psychology must make it clear to our society that the respect given to someone who is trying to climb a mountain should be different from the respect given to someone trying to climb a hill, and that the problems black youths face in education is a mountain—one for which we are all responsible.

Author's note: As a man raised in a Jewish household I have been strongly influenced by issues of social justice, which has caused me to empathize with the predicament of black athletes in America and sound this call for further analysis. From medieval times until recent history, Jews were barred from owning land and from various professions. And while Christian law prevented Christians from lending money for profit and people needed to be able to borrow money, Jews—at great risk since they could be expelled or taxed instead of repaid—filled the role of moneylenders, becoming highly proficient at this profession. Subsequently, stereotypes arose about Jews' miserliness, opportunism, and immorality concerning money. African Americans' successes in sports has an analogous history, resulting in black males being lauded for their athletic prowess while stereotyped as intellectually inferior.

My hope is that we begin to recognize the need to break down the social history of black youths and sports in America as well as the stories and histories of all subgroups of the American culture. To resonate with the painful stories and legacies of the past and present is to recognize the need for comprehensive solutions in the future.

PART VI

DOMESTIC VIOLENCE

Don't We Look Happy?

The Silence around Domestic Violence

> *There is something about American folk. They're so*
> *obsessed with comfort, convenience, and contentment.*
> *It's just like living in a hotel where the lights are always on.*
> —Cornel West

I AM LOOKING AT AN OLD PHOTO of my mother and me; her smile is forced and unnatural. It reminds me of family pictures I sometimes receive around the holiday season in which the individuals appear to have plastic smiles etched on their faces. We are all familiar with people prompting us to pose for the camera so we are photographed appearing happy by urging, "Say *cheese*. Smile." Appearing happy and smiling on a daily basis is the most approved demeanor in our society because public displays of sadness, pain, or anger make most people feel uncomfortable, ineffectual, and even critical.

Yet despite this cultural emphasis on looking happy, each year in the United States, 4 million women are victims of severe assault by boyfriends or husbands, and reported domestic violence costs over $5.8 billion, although most abuse goes unreported.[1] These statistics make it likely that each of us, at some point in our lives, will be in the role of either perpetrator, victim, doctor, nurse, friend, or family member of the abused or abusers. Many of us will play more than one of these roles in domestic violence, and as members of society, we are all responsible for facing the implications of it and trying to prevent it. As T. S. Eliot says in *Four Quartets*, "The whole earth is our hospital."[2]

A deafening silence usually surrounds acts of domestic violence because its practice is so often denied by both perpetrators and victims and because people in our society do not want to face its prevalence or implications. This is evident when looking at Web sites on domestic violence and seeing titles that include such phrases as "stopping the silence," "ending the silence," "breaking the silence," "ominous silence," "shattering the silence," and the "sin of silence." This is also reflected in book titles like *We Suffered in Silence, The Truth Behind the Walls*, or *A Deep Dark Secret*. As Susan Weitzman, Ph.D., says in her book *Not to People Like Us: Hidden Abuse in Upscale Marriage*, "If a culture's tribal rules deny a phenomenon, then it is truly bound to silence."[3] However, stopping the current epidemic of domestic violence requires that we make a hole in our wall of denial and use our collective awareness and voice to end the silence.

THE *DR. PHIL* SHOW

An episode of the *Dr. Phil* show provided a good example of how our cultural dictum to smile and look happy fosters silence around domestic violence.[4] The guests were two couples involved in domestic violence. The language they used to describe the violence reflected their denial and downplayed its seriousness. One husband described it as an "exchange of blows," neglecting to note that his blows had left his wife battered and bruised. And when he saw pictures of his wife's bruises, he said he hadn't realized it was that bad. While the husband had said many times that he would change, he never had. The wife said he had a "temper," as if to acknowledge the problem, while suggesting it was a kind of aberration instead of part of the fabric of their relationship, and stressed, "On the outside we look good." The second couple echoed this perspective. The wife, who had battered the husband, as well as the dog and the couple's child, told Dr. Phil, "From the outside, we look like a happy couple." In both cases, the couples' denial was evident.

Dr. Phil divided the responsibility for the violence between the husbands and the wives. Not one to condone denial and irresponsibility, Dr. Phil didn't let the first husband justify his actions, telling him that people turn to anger when they don't know how to express themselves in other ways. On the other hand, he wisely didn't shame the husband, wanting him to learn and change. While Dr. Phil was clearly sympathetic with the wife, he challenged her as well, telling her that victims must share responsibility for violence in their relationships. He counseled her not to accept such violence or regard it as normal. Dr. Phil also recommended that she develop a sense of self-worth so she would not allow herself to be treated so poorly and that she become less passive.

While the perpetrators of domestic violence clearly bear responsibility, many people would also conclude, like Dr. Phil, that victims share some responsibility, although not necessarily the blame. But it appears that the general public, from whom the violence is hidden, also bears a measure of responsibility by participating in the silence surrounding domestic violence in our culture.

DIVERTING ATTENTION FROM TRAUMA

In our society, we pressure, cajole, and criticize people trying to get them to smile, then we comment, "They look like such a happy couple." We even train children to smile and thus hide their true emotions. Expressions of pain, sadness, anger, grief, even genuine joy, pride, and pleasure seem to show up on an artist's film but not in the lens of commercial cameras because seeing anger and suffering in the world reminds us of our own vulnerability and culpability and so we encourage our patients, friends, family members, students, and employees to avoid showing signs of distress or pain. We medicate people to transform their feelings from sadness to happiness. We take it personally when people around us are not happy, believing we are failing to make them happy. We want facial expression to be confined to a certain form, to the point where many of us, as T. S. Eliot wrote, "prepare a face to meet the faces that you meet."[5]

The inauthentic masks we wear remind me of a newspaper story I read twenty years ago entitled "Don't I Look Happy?" about a blond-haired blue-eyed teen who had murdered his parents and siblings, smiling innocently. The article suggested it was hard for anyone to have predicted that this boy, as reflected by his appearance, would have had the potential for such horror. In connection with another incident some years later, when a television interviewer spoke to friends and neighbors about a high school shooting, they noted their surprise, saying that the shooter "always seemed like a happy boy."

There has long been resistance to acknowledging trauma, and a tendency to divert attention from it. A good example of this is the reaction to Freud's 1896 publication "The Aetiology of Hysteria," a study of six male and twelve female patients who had reported being sexually abused by either a parent or a sibling.[6] Although Freud concluded originally that the details given by the patients were too specific to have been fabricated, after negative public reaction he changed his conclusion and conjured up his theory of children's "sexual fantasies," saving people from having to deal with the horror of child abuse, the existence of which, like domestic violence, is masked by silence.

It has not been easy for our society to gain awareness of the nature and extent of abuse in families because it is an affront to everything we hold dear. Today, there are still people determined to convince the American public that others fabricate stories of their abuse with the support of unethical therapists. We idolize marriage and the family just as children idolize parents, so facing the violence that often occurs within the four walls called "home" requires breaking through the walls of our denial as much as breaking through the walls of silence built around domestic violence. For example, a student once told me how she ran to her parents' house at midnight in tears, terrified that her husband would hurt her again as he repeatedly had in the past, but instead of empathizing with her plight her parents lectured her on the sacredness of marriage and how she should do anything necessary to repair her relationship. If we remain blind by staying out of each other's business, we abdicate our role in policing violence, leaving it to escalate to the point where law enforcement officers, hospitals, or coroners get involved.

Our need to keep ourselves "looking happy" is directly related to our need to hide expressions of pain and suffering, both individually and as a society. The acclaimed psychoanalyst and author Alice Miller noted that the extent to which a society needs to maintain rigid personas—keep everything looking good—it will hide expressions of negative emotions.[7] Trauma and abuse, including domestic violence, remain hidden not only because victims don't speak up but also because society is invested in keeping them in the shadows. We all participate in such concealment, however unconsciously, and overcoming it requires us to support expression of the full range of feelings by our families, friends, and community members.

In addition to our denial and the fact that we are encouraged to hide our negative emotions behind smiles, our senses have also become less able to detect trauma, and when we do we often don't trust our impressions. We have become so invested in revealing only a narrow range of upbeat expressions that we don't notice the signs of violence, depression, stress, and distress behind the happy demeanor. We are so accustomed to people telling us they're "fine" that we no longer trust our own feelings that arise when things are not "fine." In other words, we no longer trust our distrust. Thus we don't see teenage girls on their knees throwing up in the toilet but instead admire their "nice" figures. We don't see businessmen in danger of having a heart attack as they eat and drink their way to relaxation but instead view their excesses as the privilege of success.

Even when we are in a position to witness signs of domestic violence, we do not readily notice the difference between gritted teeth and gleaming teeth, strained faces and composed faces, eyes that glare and eyes that glow. So disconnected are we that we hear only the music of our loved ones, not the dissonance reflecting the difficult feelings. So many signs and signals rush toward us like ocean waves, moment after moment, day after day, that we don't hear their roar or notice their violent drive. And our disconnectedness ensures that these dark aspects of people remain hidden.

A commercial aired by BETC Euro RSCG in Paris about domestic violence that incorporated the phrase "Silence isn't golden in domestic violence" underscores this point. The commercial showed a man going about his daily routine in his small apartment—reading a book in bed, getting ready for work, and eating toast at a kitchen table—while many sounds can be heard blending together in the background, including car alarms, a squeaky door, a dog yelping, and a woman screaming. The man relaxes into his daily life tuning them all out, including the woman screaming, who viewers discover is being beaten. Our inability to recognize signs of dissonance makes us poor witnesses of the violence in our environment. As such, we contribute to hostility, preferring to see people smile and remaining unaware of signs of their inner struggles. As Alice Miller wrote in *Thou Shalt Not Be Aware: Society's Betrayal of the Child*: "It has always been the case that it is not cruelty itself that arouses public indignation but rather calling attention to the cruelty."[8] Such lack of awareness and secrecy create an insidious relationship between victim and witness. When pain, suffering, and abuse go unconfirmed, victims aren't even sure they are being hurt because witnesses have not responded with outrage, empathy, and protection. Others conclude that the hurt they suffer is their own fault and thus inappropriately blame themselves. Thus through keeping secrets and maintaining silence victims and witnesses collude in the collective denial.

I learned early in my clinical training that many people who are depressed put on a happy face, have erect postures, and answer questions with a positive spin, as if to say, "Everything's fine; my problems are just some little blip on the screen that we shouldn't worry too much about." Fortunately there are signals of their depression—their voices may trail off, their heads may droop, or they may flop down on a chair or sofa in a way that suggests lack of energy or resignation. Of course, people may show other signs as well, such as the use of substances, outbursts in relationship, or preferences for blue music or movies. I learned that if you speak only to the upbeat part of the person, or put all your attention on trying to lift their spirits, you will never get to know what's really going on or why they are depressed. Most of the time people live in an environment, both external and internal, that is unsympathetic or even hostile to individuals feeling low, yet exploring their negative feelings provides the information needed to effect their healing.

CONCLUSION

It is important to realize that our ability to both witness and respond to the pain of others is directly related to our ability to face our own pain. If we can't look at our own traumas, then we will avert our eyes from others who have experienced trauma. Furthermore, seeing pain reminds us that we, as a society, are implicated in the cycle of domestic violence, in either big or small ways. Some of us have been hurt and not spoken up; some of us have hurt others; and many of us have simply remained blind or silent to the signs of violence around us. It is not just the abused and abuser who hide; we *all* hide—our pain, our sadness, our anger, our grief, our hurt. And it is not just the abuser and abused who hide their stories from us; we collude by not seeing.

If the whole earth is our hospital, when it comes to domestic violence we need a new intake system—one that welcomes the sharing of pains and traumas. We also need an intake environment that encourages the expression of empathy and understanding rather than pity, quick fixes, and superiority. And we need one that is smart enough to know that many people will not show all—with them we must look closely, carefully. We need to develop our personal "stethoscopes" and "X-ray machines"—our eyes, hearts, and sensitivities—so when patients come through the door we recognize them.

Let Suffering Speak
Bearing Witness to Domestic Violence

The need to let suffering speak is a condition of all truth.
—Theodore Adorno

WITNESSING THE PAIN OF OTHERS, whether it is emotional or physical, is difficult, especially when we can't help relieve it. We may wince, turn away, or feel compelled to deny or try to alleviate the pain. However, reactions like these nurture the silence around domestic violence, leading us to avoid exploring its causes and consequences. In their book *Half the Sky*, Nicholas D. Kristof and Sheryl WuDunn refer to such individual and collective denial as the "diffuse cruelty of indifference," arguing that it is indifference that allows rape, sex trafficking, and slave trading to occur around the world in epidemic proportions, citing US State Department records showing that between 600,000 and 800,000 individuals are trafficked across international borders annually, and millions of other victims are trafficked inside their own nations, 80 percent of whom are sexually exploited women and girls.[1]

Kristof and WuDunn challenge our indifference by going beyond statistics, recounting personal incidents, including the story of a woman who was forced to have sex many hours a day seven days a week; the story of a woman who was pregnant and worried about having AIDS but didn't want to take an AIDS test for fear of losing the man she loved; the story of a woman who went back to a brothel after being rescued because her captors had forced her to become addicted to drugs that she could only get there; and the story of a woman who was so publicly shamed for not being "pure" after she had been raped that she could not bear living with her family and community. The graphic details in such intimate stories of horror let suffering speak, forcing readers to see and feel others' pain.

THE *DR. PHIL* SHOW

Examining my personal reactions to an episode of the *Dr. Phil* show about domestic violence helped me learn more about the dynamics of indifference that nurtures silence around pain and violence both in myself and, by extension, the denial mechanism of others, the resistance people have to witnessing the pain caused by domestic violence and dealing with it.[2] I learned how our inability to look at our own pain makes us ill equipped to look at the pain of others, leading us to our tendency to nurture silence regarding domestic violence.Dr. Phil's guests were a man and the wife he had physically abused. The behavior of the husband and wife illustrated how even victims and perpetrators of domestic violence avoid facing its realities. They spoke about how they loved each other, the man saying that on the outside they looked like a happy couple with a good marriage. In many ways, this was reflected in their appearances. The woman's hair was neat; her clothes were attractive. She had no bruises on her face. She did not seem angry or hurt but instead forgiving of her husband's actions. For example, while she had insisted her husband leave her immediately after he had abused her, she had taken him back, saying that his pleas, promises, and explanations had been convincing. She even showed appreciation for her husband's willingness to appear on the *Dr. Phil* show and make himself vulnerable to public scrutiny and criticism. It was as if her suffering existed only in the past and the one thing left to do was figure out how to prevent such violence from happening again in the future. Listening to her, one might think that the only empathy required was for her husband taking the risk to be on the show.

However, some graphic images Dr. Phil showed of finger marks on the woman's throat and black and blue marks on her chest belied this perception. Yet even after Dr. Phil called attention to the bruises, the couple still maintained their state of denial. The wife ignored her bruises, focusing on her concern for her husband. And the husband ignored her bruises while concentrating on how good the couple's marriage had otherwise been. For me, the images of the woman's bruises challenged my indifference, like the stories of the women in *Half the Sky*, yet the power of the couple's denial led me to question whether I, too, had a tendency to ignore the violation in deference to focusing intellectually on the potential for preventing further violence.

EXPLORING THE DYNAMIC OF INDIFFERENCE

To further explore the dynamic of indifference, I later recalled the images of the woman's bruises presented on the show—the finger marks on her throat and the black and blue marks on her chest—and paid attention to my own inclination to look away. First, I flashed back to the moment the pictures had been shown on the television screen and realized that I had only given them a cursory glance. Nonetheless, I could still visualize the colors of the bruises near the woman's breasts—black, purple, blue, and red. I then noticed that even though I tried to keep my attention on the image in my mind, I was inclined to turn away, feeling the kind of queasiness I sometimes experience when seeing someone bleeding or in great pain. Examining this reaction, I became aware of tension in my body, my face forming a grimace, and my eyes squinting as if I were trying not to look.

I decided to further study my inclination to look away by forcing myself to focus on specific details of the woman's bruises—their color and their position on her body—thereby exposing myself more directly to the shadow side of her apparently happy life. Even though I considered myself someone wanting to know the inside story of news events, I wanted to escape all signs of the beatings the woman had endured. Nevertheless, I brought my focus repeatedly back to the stark reality of the bruises. Then gradually I turned to thoughts and analysis, noting that it was a relief to think and analyze as it diverted my attention from the graphic evidence of the domestic violence that had occurred. It was easier to think about how to fix the problem, prevent future abuse, or confront the abuser, imagining that I could stop the violence, than to simply be present to the woman's injured body—the marks, colors, shapes, and locations of her bruises.

As I again forced myself to focus on the bruises, I began to feel my eyes become moist, my belly grow tense, and my breath suspended until I was almost not breathing at all. Now my body seemed to be reacting more immediately to the violence documented by the images; I was in pain. I unconsciously wrapped my arms around my midsection as if to comfort myself. This eased my tension, allowing me to look at the bruises even more closely.

At this juncture, I was reminded of watching my father, in a rage, beat his fists on the body of my twelve-year-old brother while my brother crouched on his bed. Later, when my brother took his anger out on me, I was almost grateful for the experience, as it relieved me of the guilt for not having been hurt like he had been and allowed me to share the violence so I would feel close to him.

Yet again I refocused on the images of the woman's bruises. At this point it felt like my chest was caving in and my eyes blurring. "Who did this to you? Why did no one notice or help?" I protested. I imagined crying with the woman, feeling the pain of no one noticing her being beaten and stopping the violence or expressing empathy. I realized it had been necessary for me to respond to my own pain in order to actually look at the woman's wounds and empathize with her.

In addition, I understood that even though I had anticipated doing an intellectual analysis of my reactions to the images of the woman's abuse that would lead to new insights into the dynamic of indifference and to perhaps help prevent future incidents of domestic violence, my personal exploration also resulted in a heightened awareness of how connected I am to the human family by just looking and feeling. I thought of how Martin Luther King Jr. taught people to walk right into violence with a divinely inspired prayer so that others will wake up and remember their humanity.

Examining my own reactions to graphic evidence of domestic violence made it clear that if we can't truly look at injuries caused by violence then we can't truly respond to them with assistance, empathy, or preventative measures. We can only react. I could also see that our reactions to such injuries are as much about us as about the injuries of those to whom we are reacting—reflecting *our* history, *our* needs, *our* limitations, and *our* discomforts.

CONCLUSION

Considering the profusion of violence in our society, it is intriguing to speculate on the deeper psychological motivation or function of violence. Is the cycle of violence repeated from person to person and generation to generation to remind us to feel as well as think? Does its repetition actually reflect our longing to be intimate? Are we unable to face our pain until this inability becomes the bars of our cages and finally, out of desperation for truth, we break out to express our physical and emotional reality in violence?

But beyond such speculation we need to become more aware of domestic violence and find better ways to respond to it. Responding to domestic violence necessitates relating to the resulting injuries with assistance and empathy. Increasing our capacity to bear witness to others' pain—which we do by gaining more understanding of ourselves so we can better feel our connection with humanity—prevents us from being silence keepers and enables us to be healing agents.

To begin, we could take time to simply be still and deepen our understanding of ourselves, as Pablo Neruda suggests in his poem "Keeping Still":

If we were not so single-minded
about keeping our lives moving,
and for once could do nothing,
perhaps a huge silence
might interrupt this sadness
of never understanding ourselves
and of threatening ourselves with death.[3]

NOTES

Introduction

1. William Butler Yeats, from "A Dialogue of Self and Soul." Reprinted in Robert Bly, James Hillman, and Michael Meade, eds., *The Rag and Bone Shop of the Heart: Poems for Men* (New York: Harper Collins, 1992), 505–506.

2. James Hillman, *Re-Visioning Psychology* (New York: Harper & Row, 1975), 160.

3. Ibid., 145.

4. Martin Luther King Jr., "Letter from Birmingham City Jail," in *A Testament of Hope: The Essential Writings and Speeches of Martin Luther King Jr.,* James M. Washington, ed., (San Francisco: HarperSanFrancisco, 1986), 290.

5. Cornel West, *Hope on a Tightrope: Words and Wisdom* (Carlsbad, CA: Smiley Books, 2008), 210.

Call Me Crazy: Is Psychology Making Us Sick?

1. Sharon LaFraniere, "Assertive Chinese Held in Mental Wards," *New York Times*, November 12, 2010, A1.

2. "Is This Normal?" *Dr. Phil*, CBS, December 29, 2005.

3. See Arnold Mindell, *The Quantum Mind and Healing: How to Listen and Respond to Your Body's Symptoms* (Charlottesville, VA: Hampton Roads, 2004) for a full explication of Mindell's theory as it relates to the healing of physical symptoms.

Cocreating Dishonesty: Sex, Lies, and Psychology

1. United Nations Information Service, "Dramatic Increase in Methylphenidate Consumption in US: Marketing Methods Questioned," *INCB Annual Report 1995*, Background Note No. 2, February 28, 1996, accessed September 3, 2012, http://www.incb.org/pdf/e/press/1995/e_bn_02.pdf.

2. "Newlywed Dread," *Dr. Phil*, CBS, December 27, 2004.

3. Philip Zimbardo, *The Lucifer Effect: Understanding How Good People Turn Evil* (New York: Random House, 2008).

4. Jerry Fjerkenstad, personal communication, July 11, 2010.

In the Shadow of Our Judgments: Ethics and Psychology

1. See, for example, Gretchen Rubin, "I'm So Judgmental. I Want to

Conquer This! Any Suggestions?" *The Happiness Project*, posted July 13, 2010, accessed November 7, 2011, http://www.happiness. project.com/happiness_ project/2010/07im-so-judgmental-i-want-to-conquer-this-any-suggestions.html; Terry D. Cooper, *Making Judgments without Being Judgmental: Nurturing a Clear Mind and a Generous Heart* (Downers Grove, IL: InterVarsity Press, 2006); and Arnold A. Lazarus and Clifford N. Lazarus, "Are You Making Judgments . . . or Being Judgmental?" SelfGrowth.com, accessed November 7, 2011, http://self-growth.com/articles/Lazarus2html.

   2. "Judgmental People," *Dr. Phil*, CBS, March 24, 2005.

   3. Georgia Hackworth, "Stigmas, Stereotypes of Tattooing: Why the Medical Community Is to Blame," *Associated Content from Yahoo*, posted June 13, 2008, accessed November 7, 2011, http://www.associatedcontent.com/article/802129/stigmas_stereotypes_of_tattooing_why.html.

   4. *Skin Stories: The Art and Culture of Polynesian Tattoo*. First broadcast May 4, 2003 by PBS, accessed on November 7, 2011, http://www.pbs.org/skinstories/stories/index.html.

   5. Ashley Ford, "Tattoo Stereotypes," *Tattooing and Body Piercing*, accessed on November 7, 2011, http://tattooingandbodymodification.com/tattoo-stereotypes-65871a.

   6. M. M. Rooni, "Body Art—Tattoo Stereotypes," posted on October 29, 2009, accessed on November 27, 2011, http://www.associatedcontent.com/article/2331620/body_art_tattoo_stereotypes.html.

   7. Rainer Maria Rilke, "Letter to Lou Andres-Salome, January 20 and 24, 1912," *Letters of Rainer Maria Rilke*, vol. 2, 1910, 1926, trans. Jane Bannard Greene and M. D. Herter (New York: W. W. Norton, 1948).

Anger: Befriending the Beast

   1. "Ultimate Revenge," *Dr. Phil*, CBS, April 11, 2005.

   2. Emily Dickinson, "Mine Enemy Is Growing Old," *Poems: Second Series* (Boston: Roberts Brothers, 1891). Reprinted in Robert Bly, James Hillman, and Michael Meade, eds., *The Rag and Bone Shop of the Heart: Poems for Men* (New York: Harper Collins, 1992), 304.

Having It Out: Sustainable Alternatives to Compromise

   1. Rainer Maria Rilke, "The Man Watching." Reprinted in Robert Bly,

James Hillman, and Michael Meade, eds., *The Rag and Bone Shop of the Heart: Poems for Men* (New York: Harper Collins, 1992), 298.

2. "Ask Dr. Phil and Robin," *Dr. Phil*, CBS, March 16, 2005.

Relationship Conflict: What's Gender Got to Do with It?

1. John Gray, *Men Are from Mars, Women Are from Venus: A Practical Guide for Improving Communication and Getting What You Want in Your Relationships* (New York: Harper Collins, 1992).

2. "Makeover Our Marriage," *Dr. Phil*, CBS, March 18, 2005.

Rank Dynamics: The Anatomy of an Affair

1. Arnold Mindell, *Sitting in the Fire: Large Group Transformation Using Conflict and Diversity* (Portland, OR: Lao Tse Press, 1995), 49–60.

2. Timothy A. Judge and Daniel M. Cable, "The Effect of Physical Height on Workplace Success and Income: Preliminary Test of a Theoretical Model," *Journal of Applied Psychology* 89, no. 3 (June 2004): 428–41.

3. US Government Accountability Office (GAO) Report GAO-04-35, *Women's Earnings.* The weekly earnings of full-time working women were about three-fourths of men's during 2001. Even accounting for factors such as occupation, industry, race, marital status, and job tenure, reports the GAO, working women today earn an average of 80 cents for every dollar earned by their male counterparts. Posted October 31, 2003, accessed June 5, 2012, http://www.gao.gov/products/GAO-04-35.

4. Lisa Cullen, "Do Women Bully Women at Work?" Time data from Dr. Gary Namie, director of the Workplace Bullying Institute. Posted March 26, 2008, accessed June 5, 2012, http://moneyland.time.com/2008/03/26/do_women_bully_wom_at_work/.

5. Robert W. Fuller, *Somebodies and Nobodies: Overcoming the Abuse of Rank* (Gabriola Island, BC: New Society, 2003), 2–11.

6. "Torn between Two Lovers—Part 1," *Dr. Phil*, CBS, August 3, 2005.

Married to Dieting: Banking on Failure

1. Janet Melcher and Gerald J. Bostwick Jr., "The Obese Client: Myths, Facts, Assessment, and Intervention," *Health and Social Work* 23, no. 3 (1998): 195–202.

2. Monica Persson, "Fat and Feminist Large Women's Health Experiences," Feminist Women's Health Center, 1996, accessed October 31, 2011, http://www.fwhc.org/health/fatfem.htm.

3. Ibid.

4. Danice K. Eaton, Richard Lowry, Nancy D. Brener, Deborah A. Galuska, and Alex E. Crosby, "Associations of Body Mass Index and Perceived Weight with Suicide Ideation and Suicide Attempts among US High School Students," *Archives of Pediatrics & Adolescent Medicine* 159, no. 6 (2005): 513–19.

5. L. M. Mellin, C. E. Irwin, and S. Scully, "Disordered Eating Characteristics in Girls: A Survey of Middle-Class Children," *Journal of the American Dietetic Association* (1992): 851–53.

6. Catherine M. Shisslak, Marjorie Crago, and Linda S. Estes, "The Spectrum of Eating Disturbances," *International Journal of Eating Disorders* 18, no. 3 (1995): 209-19.

7. Ibid., 213.

8. "Eating Order Statistics," South Carolina Department of Mental Health, accessed October 31, 2011, http://www.state.sc.us/dmh/anorexia/statistics.htm.

9. Naomi Wolf, *The Beauty Myth: How Images of Beauty Are Used against Women* (New York: Harper Perennial, 2002 [1991]), 229.

10. Hilary Rowland, "Obsessed with Thin: Has the Media Gone Too Far?" *Urbanette* Magazine, accessed October 31, 2011, http://www.urbanette.com/obsessed-with-thin-media-gone-too-far/.

11. A. E. Andersen and L. DiDomenico, "Diet vs. Shape Content of Popular Male and Female Magazines: A Dose-Response Relationship to the Incidence of Eating Disorders?" *International Journal of Eating Disorders* 11 (1992): 238–87.

12. Marketdata Enterprises, "The US Weight Loss & Diet Control Market," 11th ed., posted May 1, 2011, accessed October 31, 2011, http://www.marketresearch.com/Marketdata-Enterprises-Inc-v416/Weight-Loss-Diet-Control-11th-6314539/.

13. Jane R. Hirschmann and Carol H. Munter, *Overcoming Overeating: How to Break the Diet/Binge Cycle and Live a Healthier, More Satisfying Life* (Philadelphia: Da Capo Press, 2008 [1998]).

14. Amanda Spake, "Stop Dieting! Forget the Scale, the Calorie Counting, and Forbidden Foods. They May Be Doing More Harm Than Good," *US News*

& World Report, posted January 8, 2006, accessed October 31, 2011, http://health.usnews.com/usnews/health/articles/060116/16diet.htm.

15. Traci Mann, A. Janet Tomiyama, Erika Westling, Ann-Marie Lew, Barbra Samuels, and Jason Chatman, "Medicare's Search for Effective Obesity Treatments: Diets Are Not the Answer," *American Psychologist* 62, no. 3 (2007): 220–33.

16. Glenn A. Gaesser, *Big Fat Lies: The Truth about Your Weight and Your Health* (Carlsbad, CA: Gürze Books, 2002 [1996]), 77.

17. "Overweight Brides," *Dr. Phil*, CBS, January 12, 2005.

18. Hirschmann and Munter, *Overcoming Overeating*

Diets As Koans: Zen and the Art of Weight Loss

1. "Overweight Brides," *Dr. Phil*, CBS, January 12, 2005.

Can I Get a Witness? Taking a Stand against Assaults on Body Image

1. "Overweight Brides," *Dr. Phil*, CBS, January 12, 2005.

2. W. E. B. Du Bois, *The Souls of Black Folk* (New York: Gramercy Books, 1994).

3. Casey L. Augustus-Horvath and Tracy L. Tylka, "A Test and Extension of Objectification Theory As It Predicts Disordered Eating: Does Women's Age Matter?" *Journal of Counseling Psychology* 56, no. 2: 253–65.

4. Ibid.

5. Ibid.

6. Diane M. Quinn, Rachel W. Kallen, Jean M. Twenge, and Barbara L. Fredrickson, "The Disruptive Effect of Self-Objectification on Performance," *Psychology of Women Quarterly* 30, no. 1: 59–64.

7. Barbara Frederickson and Tomi-Ann Roberts, "Objectification Theory: Toward Understanding Women's Lived Experiences and Mental Health Risks," *Psychology of Women Quarterly* 21, no. 2: 173-206.

8. Rachel D. Peterson, Karen P. Grippo, and Stacey Tantleff-Dunn, "Empowerment and Powerlessness: A Closer Look at the Relationship between Feminism, Body Image and Eating Disturbance," *Sex Roles* 58, nos. 9 and 10: 639-48.

9. See, for example, Anne Burt and Christina Baker Kline, eds., *About Face: Women Write about What They See When They Look in the Mirror* and Margo Maine and Joe Kelly, *The Body Myth: Adult Women and the Pressure to be Perfect*.

Substances As Allies: The Urge for Altered States

1. R. L. Hubbard, S. G. Craddock, P. M. Flynn, J. Anderson, and R. M. Etheridge, Substance Abuse and Mental Health Services Administration (SAMHSA) and Center for Substance Abuse Treatment (CSAT), 1997, The National Treatment Improvement Evaluation Study (NTIES).

2. Nora D. Volkow, M.D., Director, National Institute on Drug Abuse, National Institute of Health, Department of Health and Human Services, "Measuring the Effectiveness of Drug Addiction Treatment." Statement before the House Committee on Government Reform Subcommittee on Criminal Justice, Drug Policy and Human Resources, United States House of Representatives, posted March 30, 2004; revised November 1, 2004, http://www.hhs.gov/asl/testify/t040330c.html.

3. B.T. Jones and J. McMahon, "Negative and Positive Alcohol Expectancies as Predictors of Abstinence after Discharge from a Residential Treatment Program: A One-month and Three-month Follow-up Study of Men," *Journal of Studies on Alcohol* 55 (1994): 543-48.

4. N. S. Miller and N. G. Hoffman, "Addictions Treatment Outcomes," *Alcohol Treatment Quarterly* 12 (1995): 41–55.; J. Chappel, "Long-Term Recovery from Alcoholism," *Psychiatric Clinics of North America* (1993): 177–89.

5. G. DeLeon and S. Schwartz, "The Therapeutic Community: What Are the Retention Rates?" *American Journal of Drug and Alcohol Abuse* 10 (1984): 267–84.

6. Volkow, "Measuring the Effectiveness."

7. N. S. Miller and M. S. Gold, "The Role of the Psychiatrist in Treatment of Relapse in Addictive Disorders," *Behavior Therapy* 25 (1995): 673–78.

8. See, for example, Narconon International, http://addiction.narcononrehab.com/drug-addiction/top-ten-reasons-people-use-drugs/ and Pace University Counseling Center, http://www.pace.edu/counseling-center/line-resources/about-alcohol-and-other-drugs.

9. Richard Fields, *Drugs in Perspective: Causes, Assessment, Family, Prevention, Intervention, and Treatment,* 7th ed. (New York: McGraw-Hill, 2010), 4.

10. Ibid., 6.

11. Ibid., 25.

12. "Addiction Resolutions," *Dr. Phil,* CBS, January 5, 2005.

Making Me Over: Obsessing about Obsessions

1. "Celebrity Obsessed," *Dr. Phil*, CBS, June 24, 2005.

All Together Now: Appreciating Family Diversity

1. "Black Sheep of the Family," *Dr. Phil*, CBS, June 20, 2005.

2. Salvador Minuchin, *Families and Family Therapy* (Cambridge, MA: Harvard University Press: 1974), 110.

Passion through the Ages: Sex and Shame

1. "Ask Dr. Phil about Sex," *Dr. Phil*, CBS, August 19, 2005.

2. Alfred Kinsey, W. Pomeroy, C. Martin, and P. Gebhard, *Sexual Behavior in the Human Female* (Philadelphia: Saunders, 1953).

3. Arnold Mindell, *The Dreammaker's Apprentice: The Psychological and Spiritual Interpretation of Dreams* (Portland, OR: Lao Tse Press, 2008 [2001]).

Breaking It Down: Black Youths, Sports, and Education

1. Ken Burns, *Unforgivable Blackness: The Rise and Fall of Jack Johnson*, PBS, 2005.

2. Ibid.

3. Barak Y. Orbach, *The Johnson-Jeffries Fight and Censorship of Black Supremacy*. *NYU Journal of Law and Liberty* 8 (July 22, 2010), 270, accessed August 27, 2012, http://www.law.nyu.edu/ecm_dlv3/groups/public/@nyu_law_website__journals__journal_of_law_and_liberty/documents/documents/ecm_pro_066938.pdf.

4. "Coach Carter," *Dr. Phil*, CBS, January 11, 2005.

5. Jonathan Kozol, *Savage Inequalities: Children in America's Schools* (New York: Crown Publisher, 1991); see also "Achievement Gap," *Education Week*, posted August 3, 2004, updated July 7, 2011, accessed August 27, 2012, http://edweek.org/ew/issues/achievement-gap/.

6. Richard Whitmire, "Time Is Running Out on Urban Schools," *DLC (Democratic Leadership Council)*. As printed in *Blueprint Magazine*. Posted July 29, 2002, accessed August 27, 2012, http://www.dlc.org/ndol_ci1977.html?kaid=110&subid=136&contentid=250686.

7. Erica Frankenberg, Chungmei Lee, and Gary Orfield, *A Multiracial Society with Segregated Schools: Are We Losing the Dream?* (Cambridge, MA: Harvard University, 2003). Report by the Civil Rights Project.

8. Kozol, *Savage Inequalities*, 234–37.

9. M. Planty and J.F. DeVoe, *An Examination of the Conditions of School Facilities Attended by 10th-Grade Students in 2002* (NCES 2006-302) US Department of Education, National Center for Education Statistics (Washington, DC: US Government Printing Office, 2005), 4.

10. Anthony P. Carnevale, Jeff Strohl, and Michelle Melton, *What's It Worth? The Economic Value of College Majors.* Report by Center on Education and the Workforce (Washington, DC: Georgetown University, 2011).

11. Kevin Chappell, "One-on-One with Bill Gates: 'Why Aren't There Protests Every Day?'" *Ebony Magazine.* Accessed November 7, 2011, http://stage.ebonyjet.com/CurrentIssue/Oct2011_BillGates.aspx.

12. Nathan McCall, *What's Going On: Personal Essays* (New York: Random House, 1997).

13. Michael Eric Dyson, *Open Mike: Reflections on Philosophy, Race, Sex, Culture and Religion* (New York: Basic Civitas Books, 2003), 255.

Don't We Look Happy? The Silence around Domestic Violence

1. Department of Health and Human Services, *Costs of Intimate Partner Violence against Women in the United States* (Atlanta: National Center for Injury Prevention and Control, 2003), 2.

2. T. S. Eliot, *Four Quartets* (New York: Mariner Books, 1968), 30.

3. Susan Weitzman, *Not to People Like Us: Hidden Abuse in Upscale Marriage* (New York: Basic Books, 2001), 8.

4. "Dr. Phil Takes on Abusers," *Dr. Phil*, CBS, June 7, 2005.

5. T. S. Eliot, "The Love Song of J. Alfred Prufrock," in *Prufrock and Other Observations* (New York: Knopf, 1920). Posted on Bartleby.com, accessed August 27, 2012, http://www.bartleby.com/198/1.html/.

6. Sigmund Freud, "The Aetiology of Hysteria," *The Standard Edition of the Complete Psychological Works of Sigmund Freud,* vol. 3, 1893–1899, (Early Psycho-Analytic Publications, 1896): 187–221.

7. Alice Miller, *Thou Shalt Not Be Aware: Society's Betrayal of the Child* (New York: Farrar, Straus and Giroux, 1981), 190.

8. Ibid.

Let Suffering Speak: Bearing Witness to Domestic Violence

1. Nicholas D. Kristof and Sheryl WuDunn, *Half the Sky: Turning Oppression into Opportunity for Women Worldwide* (New York: Knopf, 2009), 10.

2. "Dr. Phil Takes on Abusers," *Dr. Phil*, CBS, June 7, 2005.

3. Pablo Neruda, "Keeping Still," in *Extravagaria*, ed. Alastair Reid (London: Jonathan Cape, 1972), 28.

BIBLIOGRAPHY

"About Alcohol and Other Drugs." Pace University Counseling Center. Accessed August 27, 2012. http://www.pace.edu/counseling-center/line-resources/about-alcohol-and-other-drugs.

"Achievement Gap." *Education Week.* Posted August 3, 2004. Updated July 7, 2011. Accessed August 27, 2012. http://www.edweek.org/ew/issues/achievement-gap/.

"Addiction Resolutions." *Dr. Phil.* CBS. January 5, 2005.

Andersen, A. E., and L. DiDomenico. "Diet vs. Shape Content of Popular Male and Female Magazines: A Dose-Response Relationship to the Incidence of Eating Disorders?" *International Journal of Eating Disorders* 11 (1992): 238–87.

"Ask Dr. Phil about Sex." *Dr. Phil.* CBS. August 19, 2005.

"Ask Dr. Phil and Robin." *Dr. Phil.* CBS. March 16, 2005.

Augustus-Horvath, Casey L. and Tracy L. Tylka. "A Test and Extension of Objectification Theory As It Predicts Disordered Eating: Does Women's Age Matter?" *Journal of Counseling Psychology* 56, no. 2: 253–65.

"Black Sheep of the Family." *Dr. Phil.* CBS. June 20, 2005.

Burns, Ken. *Unforgivable Blackness: The Rise and Fall of Jack Johnson.* PBS. 2005.

Burt, Anne, and Christina Baker Kline, eds. *About Face: Women Write about What They See When They Look in the Mirror.* Berkeley: Seal Press, 2008.

Carnevale, Anthony, Jeff Strohl, and Michelle Melton. *What's It Worth? The Economic Value of College Majors.* Report by Center on Education and the Workforce. Washington, DC: Georgetown University, 2011.

"Celebrity Obsessed." *Dr. Phil.* CBS. June 24, 2005.

Chappel, J. "Long-Term Recovery from Alcoholism." *Psychiatric Clinics of North America* (1993): 177–89.

Chappell, Kevin. "One-on-One with Bill Gates: 'Why Aren't There Protests Every Day?'" *Ebony Magazine.* Accessed November 7, 2011. http://stage.ebonyjet.com/CurrentIssue/Oct2011_BillGates.aspx.

"Coach Carter." *Dr. Phil.* CBS. January 11, 2005.

Cooper, Terry D. *Making Judgments without Being Judgmental: Nurturing a Clear Mind and a Generous Heart.* Downers Grove, IL: InterVarsity Press, 2006.

Cullen, Lisa. "Do Women Bully Women at Work?" *Workplace Bullying Institute.* Posted March 26, 2008. Accessed June 5, 2012. http://moneyland.time.com/2008/03/26/do_women_bully_wom_at_work/.

DeLeon, G., and S. Schwartz. "The Therapeutic Community: What Are the Retention Rates?" *American Journal of Drug and Alcohol Abuse* 10 (1984): 267–84.

Department of Health and Human Services. *Costs of Intimate Partner Violence against Women in the United States.* Atlanta: National Center for Injury Prevention and Control, March 2003.

Dickinson, Emily. "Mine Enemy Is Growing Old." *Poems: Second Series.* Boston: Roberts Brothers, 1891. Reprinted in Robert Bly, James Hillman, and Michael Meade, eds. *The Rag and Bone Shop of the Heart: Poems for Men.* New York: Harper Collins, 1992.

"Dr. Phil Takes on Abusers." *Dr. Phil.* CBS. June 7, 2005.

Du Bois, W. E. B. *The Souls of Black Folk.* New York: Gramercy Books, 1994.

Dyson, Michael Eric. *Open Mike: Reflections on Philosophy, Race, Sex, Culture and Religion.* New York: Basic Civitas Books, 2003.

"Eating Order Statistics." South Carolina Department of Mental Health. Accessed October 31, 2011, http://www.state.sc.us/dmh/anorexia/statistics.htm.

Eaton, Danice K., Richard Lowry, Nancy D. Brener, Deborah A. Galuska, and Alex E. Crosby. "Associations of Body Mass Index and Perceived Weight with Suicide Ideation and Suicide Attempts among US High School Students." *Archives of Pediatrics & Adolescent Medicine* 159, no. 6 (2005): 513–19.

Eliot, T. S. *Four Quartets.* New York: Mariner Books, 1968.

———. "The Love Song of J. Alfred Prufrock." *Prufrock and Other Observations.* New York: A.A. Knopf, 1920. Posted on Bartleby.com. Accessed August 27, 2012. http://www.bartleby.com/198/1.html/.

Fields, Richard. *Drugs in Perspective: Causes, Assessment, Family, Prevention, Intervention, and Treatment,* 7th ed. New York: McGraw-Hill, 2010.

Fjerkenstad, Jerry. Personal communication. July 11, 2010.

Ford, Ashley. "Tattoo Stereotypes." *Tattooing and Body Piercing.* Accessed November 7, 2011. http://tattooingandbodymodification.com/tattoo-stereotypes-65871a.

Frankenberg, Erica, Chungmei Lee, and Gary Orfield. *A Multiracial Society with Segregated Schools: Are We Losing the Dream?* Cambridge, MA: Harvard University, January 2003.

Frederickson, Barbara, and Tomi-Ann Roberts. "Objectification Theory: Toward Understanding Women's Lived Experiences and Mental Health Risks." *Psychology of Women Quarterly* 21, no. 2: 173–206.

Freud, Sigmund. "The Aetiology of Hysteria." *The Standard Edition of the Complete Psychological Works of Sigmund Freud*, vol. 3, 1893–1899. Early Psycho-Analytic Publications, 1896.

Fuller, Robert W. *Somebodies and Nobodies: Overcoming the Abuse of Rank*. Gabriola Island, BC: New Society Publishers, 2003.

Gaesser, Glenn A. *Big Fat Lies: The Truth about Your Weight and Your Health*. Carlsbad, CA: Gürze Books, 2002 [1996].

Gray, John. *Men Are from Mars, Women Are from Venus: A Practical Guide for Improving Communication and Getting What You Want in Your Relationships*. New York: Harper Collins, 1992.

Hackworth, Georgia. "Stigmas, Stereotypes of Tattooing: Why the Medical Community Is to Blame." *Associated Content from Yahoo*. Posted June 13, 2008. Accessed November 7, 2011. http://www.associatedcontent.com/article/802129/stigmas_stereotypes_of_tattooing_why.html.

Hillman, James. *Re-Visioning Psychology*. New York: Harper & Row, 1975.

Hirschmann, Jane R., and Carol H. Munter. *Overcoming Overeating: How to Break the Diet/Binge Cycle and Live a Healthier, More Satisfying Life*. Philadelphia: Da Capo Press, 2008 [1998].

Hubbard, R. L, S. G. Craddock, P. M. Flynn, J. Anderson, and R. M. Etheridge. "The National Treatment Improvement Evaluation Study (NTIES)." Substance Abuse and Mental Health Services Administration (SAMHSA). Rockville, MD: Center for Substance Abuse Treatment, 1997.

"Is This Normal?" *Dr. Phil*. CBS. December 29, 2005.

Jones, B. T., and J. McMahon. "Negative and Positive Alcohol Expectancies As Predictors of Abstinence after Discharge from a Residential Treatment Program: A One-Month and Three-Month Follow-Up Study of Men." *Journal of Studies on Alcohol* 55 (1994): 543–48.

Judge, Timothy A., and Daniel M. Cable. "The Effect of Physical Height on Workplace Success and Income: Preliminary Test of a Theoretical Model." *Journal of Applied Psychology* 89, no. 3 (June 2004): 428–41.

"Judgmental People." *Dr. Phil*. CBS. March 24, 2005.

King Jr., Martin Luther. "Letter from Birmingham City Jail." In *A Testament of Hope: The Essential Writings and Speeches of Martin Luther King Jr.*, edited by James M. Washington, 289-302. San Francisco: HarperSanFrancisco, 1986.

Kinsey, Alfred, W. Pomeroy, C. Martin, and P. Gebhard. *Sexual Behavior in the Human Female.* Philadelphia: Saunders, 1953.

Kozol, Jonathan. *Savage Inequalities: Children in America's Schools.* New York: Crown, 1991.

Kristof, Nicholas D., and Sheryl WuDunn. *Half the Sky: Turning Oppression into Opportunity for Women Worldwide.* New York: Knopf, 2009.

LaFraniere, Sharon. "Assertive Chinese Held in Mental Wards." *New York Times,* November 12, 2010.

Lazarus, Arnold A., and Clifford N. Lazarus. "Are You Making Judgments . . . or Being Judgmental?" *SelfGrowth.com.* Accessed November 7, 2011. http:// selfgrowth.com/articles/Lazarus2html.

Maine, Margo, and Joe Kelly. *The Body Myth: Adult Women and the Pressure to Be Perfect.* Hoboken, NJ: John Wiley & Sons, 2005.

"Makeover Our Marriage." *Dr. Phil.* CBS. March 18, 2005.

Mann, Traci, A. Janet Tomiyama, Erika Westling, Ann-Marie Lew, Barbra Samuels, and Jason Chatman. "Medicare's Search for Effective Obesity Treatments: Diets Are Not the Answer." *American Psychologist* 62, no. 3 (2007): 220–33.

Marketdata Enterprises. "The US Weight Loss & Diet Control Market," 11th ed. Biennial study. Posted May 1, 2011. Accessed October 31, 2011. http:// www.marketresearch.com/Marketdata-Enterprises-Inc-v416/Weight-Loss-Diet-Control-11th-6314539/.

McCall, Nathan. *What's Going On: Personal Essays.* New York: Random House, 1997.

Melcher, Janet, and Gerald J. Bostwick Jr. "The Obese Client: Myths, Facts, Assessment, and Intervention." *Health and Social Work* 23, no. 3 (1998): 195–202.

Mellin, L. M., C. E. Irwin, and S. Scully. "Disordered Eating Characteristics in Girls: A Survey of Middle-Class Children." *Journal of the American Dietetic Association* (1992): 851–53.

Miller, Alice. *Thou Shalt Not Be Aware: Society's Betrayal of the Child.* New York: Farrar, Straus and Giroux, 1981.

Miller, N. S., and M. S. Gold. "The Role of the Psychiatrist in Treatment of Relapse in Addictive Disorders." *Behavior Therapy* 25 (1995): 673–78.

Miller, N. S., and N. G. Hoffman. "Addictions Treatment Outcomes." *Alcohol Treatment Quarterly* 12 (1995): 41–55.

Mindell, Arnold. *The Dreammaker's Apprentice: The Psychological and Spiritual Interpretation of Dreams.* Portland, OR: Lao Tse Press, 2008 [2001].

———. *The Quantum Mind and Healing: How to Listen and Respond to Your Body's Symptoms*. Charlottesville, VA: Hampton Roads, 2004.

———. *Sitting in the Fire: Large Group Transformation Using Conflict and Diversity.* Portland, OR: Lao Tse Press, 1995.

Minuchin, Salvador. *Families and Family Therapy.* Cambridge, MA: Harvard University Press, 1974.

Neruda, Pablo. "Keeping Still." In *Extravagaria,* ed. by Alastair Reid. London: Jonathan Cape, 1972.

"Newlywed Dread." *Dr. Phil.* CBS. December 27, 2004.

Orbach, Barak Y. "The Johnson-Jeffries Fight and Censorship of Black Supremacy." *NYU Journal of Law and Liberty* 8 (July 22, 2010): 270–346. Accessed August 27, 2012. http://www.law.nyu.edu/ecm_dlv3/groups/public/@ nyu_law_website__journals__journal_of_law_and_liberty/documents/ documents/ecm_pro_066938.pdf.

"Overweight Brides." *Dr. Phil.* CBS. January 12, 2005.

Persson, Monica. "Fat and Feminist Large Women's Health Experiences." Feminist Women's Health Center. Posted 1996. Accessed October 31, 2011. http:// www.fwhc.org/health/fatfem.htm.

Peterson, Rachel D., Karen P. Grippo, and Stacey Tantleff-Dunn. "Empowerment and Powerlessness: A Closer Look at the Relationship between Feminism, Body Image and Eating Disturbance." *Sex Roles* 58, nos. 9 and 10: 639–648.

Planty, M., and J. F. DeVoe. *An Examination of the Conditions of School Facilities Attended by 10th-Grade Students in 2002* (NCES 2006-302). U.S. Department of Education, National Center for Education Statistics. Washington, DC: US Government Printing Office, 2005.

Quinn, Diane M., Rachel W. Kallen, Jean M. Twenge, and Barbara L. Fredrickson. "The Disruptive Effect of Self-Objectification on Performance." *Psychology of Women Quarterly* 30, no. 1: 59–64.

Rilke, Rainer Maria. "Letter to Lou Andres-Salome, January 20 and 24, 1912." *Letters of Rainer Maria Rilke.* vol. II, 1910 1926. New York: W. W. Norton, 1948.

———. "The Man Watching." Reprinted in Robert Bly, James Hillman, and Michael Meade, eds. *The Rag and Bone Shop of the Heart: Poems for Men.* New York: Harper Collins, 1992.

Rooni, M. M. "Body Art—Tattoo Stereotypes." Posted October 29, 2009. Accessed November 27, 2011. http://www.associatedcontent.com/article/2331620/body_art_tattoo_stereotypes.html.

Rowland, Hilary. "Obsessed with Thin: Has the Media Gone Too Far?" *Urbanette Magazine*. Accessed October 31, 2011, http://www.urbanette.com/obsessed-with-thin-media-gone-too-far/.

Rubin, Gretchen. "I'm So Judgmental. I Want to Conquer This! Any Suggestions?" *The Happiness Project*. Posted July 13, 2010. Accessed November 7, 2011. http://www.happiness project.com/happiness_project/2010/07im-so-judgmental-i-want-to-conquer-this-any-suggestions.html.

Shisslak, Catherine M., Marjorie Crago, and Linda S. Estes. "The Spectrum of Eating Disturbances." *International Journal of Eating Disorders* 18, no. 3 (1995): 209–219.

"Skin Stories: The Art and Culture of Polynesian Tattoo." PBS. First broadcast May 4, 2003. Accessed November 7, 2011. http://www.pbs.org/skinstories/stories/index.html.

Spake, Amanda. "Stop Dieting! Forget the Scale, the Calorie Counting, and Forbidden Foods. They May Be Doing More Harm Than Good." *US News & World Report*. Posted January 8, 2006. Accessed October 31, 2011. http://health.usnews.com/usnews/health/articles/060116/16diet.htm.

"Top Ten Reasons People Use Drugs." Narconon International. Posted August 12, 2009. Accessed August 27, 2012. http://addiction.narcononrehab.com/drug-addiction/top-ten-reasons-people-use-drugs/.

"Torn between Two Lovers—Part 1." *Dr. Phil*. CBS. August 3, 2005.

"Ultimate Revenge." *Dr. Phil*. CBS. April 11, 2005.

United Nations Information Service. "Dramatic Increase in Methylphenidate Consumption in US: Marketing Methods Questioned." *INCB Annual Report 1995, Background Note No. 2*. February 28, 1996. Accessed September 3, 2012. http://www.incb.org/pdf/e/press/1995/e_bn_02.pdf.

Volkow, Nora D. "Measuring the Effectiveness of Drug Addiction Treatment." Statement before the the House Committee on Government Reform, Subcommittee on Criminal Justice, Drug Policy and Human Resources,United States House of Representatives. Posted March 30, 2004. Revised November 1, 2004. http://www.hhs.gov/asl/testify/t040330c.html.

Weitzman, Susan. *Not to People Like Us: Hidden Abuse in Upscale Marriage.* New York: Basic Books, 2001.

West, Cornel. *Hope on a Tightrope: Words and Wisdom.* Carlsbad, CA: Smiley Books, 2008.

Whitmire, Richard. "Time Is Running Out on Urban Schools." *Blueprint Magazine.* Posted July 29, 2002. Accessed August 27, 2012. http://www.dlc. org/ndol_ci1977.html?kaid=110&subid=136&contentid=250686.

Wolf, Naomi. *The Beauty Myth: How Images of Beauty Are Used against Women.* New York: Harper Perennial, 2002 [1991].

"Women's Earnings." US Government Accountability Office (GAO). Report GAO-04-35. Posted Oct. 31, 2003. Accessed June 5, 2012. http://www. gao.gov/products/GAO-04-35.

Yeats, William Butler. "A Dialogue of Self and Soul." In *The Rag and Bone Shop of the Heart: Poems for Men,* edited by Robert Bly, James Hillman, and Michael Meade. New York: Harper Collins, 1992.

Zimbardo, Philip. *The Lucifer Effect: Understanding How Good People Turn Evil.* New York: Random House, 2008.

INDEX

About the Author

D AVID BEDRICK, J.D., DIPL.PW, is a teacher, counselor, attorney, organizational consultant, and writer. His broad range of knowledge
is apparent in the scope of topics he taught while on the faculty of the
University of Phoenix, including courses on philosophy (critical thinking
and ethics) and psychology (addictions and dependencies, negotiation
and mediation, clinical interviewing, cultural diversity, ethics in human
services, and group work), as well as employment law and conflict management in the MBA program. His love of diverse audiences is apparent
in the variety of venues where he has taught, such as the U.S. Navy, 3M, the
American Society of Training and Development, the Process Work Institute,
psychological associations, and small groups focusing on personal growth.
In 2005, he received the Faculty of the Year Award in Human Services
award from the University of Phoenix.

As a practitioner of process-oriented psychology, a branch of Jungian
psychology, he has worked with groups, couples, and individuals for nearly
twenty years. His graduate work in psychology at the University of Minnesota and clinical training at the Process Work Institute, where he is a

diplomate and teacher as well as serving on the ethics committee and on the advisory board for the master's program in conflict resolution, provided the basis for the "love-based psychology" he advocates in this book.

Bedrick has also been a member of the Oregon State Bar since 1999, when he graduated first in his class from Lewis and Clark Law School. His mastery in psychology, conflict resolution, and law led to a focus on family law with a specialty in resolving intractable custody disputes. His dedication to serving the community was acknowledged in 2003 by the Oregon State Bar, which presented him with the Award for the Highest Level of Pro Bono Service.

In 1982, he cofounded the organizational consulting firm Applied Personnel Technologies, Inc. (APT), which utilized cutting-edge expertise in psychometrics to build a survey-feedback system for analyzing and changing organizational cultures, a system that has since been used by such organizations as Honeywell, Polaroid, First Bank, Cray Research, Northwestern National Life, and Control Data Corporation. Bedrick has also served as a team builder and management trainer to organizations ranging from local women's shelters and United Way to Fortune 500 companies. In 1986, he won the American Society of Training and Developments' Professional Excellence Award for Technological Innovation in employee development.

Currently, he maintains a practice as a counselor and coach for individuals and groups, and speaks on topics ranging from ethics, diversity, relationships, and conflict facilitation to dreams, diet, body image, anger, and shame.